HISTORIC CRIMES & JUSTICE
IN PORTSMOUTH
NEW HAMPSHIRE

DR. DAVID FERLAND

Charleston   London

THE
History
PRESS

Published by The History Press
Charleston, SC 29403
www.historypress.net

Copyright © 2014 by Dr. David Ferland
All rights reserved

First published 2014

Manufactured in the United States

ISBN 978.1.62619.237.9

Library of Congress CIP data applied for.

To the Portsmouth Police officers of the past, present and into the future…the guardians of Portsmouth, New Hampshire.[1]

Portsmouth Police patrol officer's badge. *Image taken by Sergeant Christopher Roth; property of the Portsmouth Police Department, used with permission.*

CONTENTS

INTRODUCTION

Police officers are storytellers. The best can relate the facts of a past event in a way that transports their audience back to the scene with them. People like stories, and cops like telling them. I wrote this early history of crime, punishment and the Portsmouth Police Department as a story. My investigative discipline, honed by thirty years of serving as a police officer, aided in this factual presentation of compelling crime stories.

The histories of Portsmouth crime and the Portsmouth Police Department are a great way to learn about the greater histories of crime, punishment and the evolution of police. Justice in the seaport city mirrors the history of justice as it relates to the early colonial days and the formation of constables and sheriffs. Portsmouth conducted several hangings, performed frequent public whippings at the town pump and had problems with witches long before the famed Salem, Massachusetts witch trials. Portsmouth is a great place to follow the establishment of police departments because it has one of the earliest formal police departments in the country and successfully moved through the various progressive reform movements. Portsmouth can also be used as a case study when investigating police corruption because it contended with a city marshal who was "on the take" and drunken cops who looked the other way from world-famous brothels.

Family members and historians such as Kimberly Crisp, Ray Brighton, Carolyn Marvin and J. Dennis Robinson have added to Portsmouth's history by uncovering seemingly lost or deeply buried artifacts that help to tell the story. This criminal account is as accurate as I can make it,

Downtown Portsmouth showing the deep-water harbor and the Portsmouth Naval Shipyard. *Image property of the Portsmouth Police Department, used with permission.*

but I find new sources of information almost every day. These stories are not just a compilation of fact, legend and lore but also a police officer's critical investigation designed to allow you to conduct your own analysis and draw your own conclusions. It represents the most probable account of crime, punishment and the early history of the Portsmouth, New Hampshire Police Department.

Note: The author's proceeds from this book will be donated to the Portsmouth, New Hampshire Police Explorers—the next generation of police officers.

INDIANS AND EXILES

For twelve thousand years, people have lived in what is now Portsmouth, New Hampshire, but it has been for only the past four hundred years that we have needed anything close to law enforcement or police officers. Early American Indians roamed the primeval forests of Portsmouth from the Merrimac River Valley in present-day Massachusetts all the way to the Labrador Sea in present-day Canada. Nomadic and in constant search of food, they lived in small tribes that often numbered just a few families.

For them, social discipline was nothing more than an informal extension of basic family management. They were strong believers in a spiritual

Abenaki encampment, by Coley Cleary. *Author's collection.*

Abenaki family, by Coley Cleary. *Author's collection.*

afterlife with narrated canons being told and enforced by the tribal elders. Rules were based on their deep beliefs of harmony, justice and balance, and the early "policing" of these rules was left to everyone within the tribe, especially the elders. Threats to their immediate safety came more from nature in the form of weather and animals than from other human beings. Mother Nature was harder to tame than the few people who were generally born into the tribe and conformed to rules by lifelong assimilation. The rules were formed around the means for survival, with further reinforcement of these rules coming from spiritual beliefs.

Belonging to a strong collective group was mutually beneficial for individual survival. All members of the tribe were expected to render aid to one another in times of need. Conversely, when a member of the group misbehaved or otherwise threatened its stasis, the other members countered quickly because their individual survival could be in jeopardy in the face of nonconformist behaviors. Banishment from the tribe was the established punishment for those individuals who would not conform to the group norms.

English captain John Mason of the Laconia Company was granted the land between the Merrimac and Kennebec Rivers in 1622, and in 1623, the first permanent European settlement of one hundred people was established at Odiorne Point, where Mason's Hall was built. Soon, hundreds of "exiles" from the

European explorer, by Coley Cleary. *Author's collection.*

Massachusetts Bay Colony arrived. Places like Plimoth were being settled by the Puritan Pilgrims, who would order the removal of people who did not conform to their strict religious rules. The Royal Commission of 1664–66 described the first eastern fishermen as "never [having] any government among them; most of them are such as have fled from other places to avoid justice. Some here are of the opinion that as many men may share a woman as they do a boat, and some have done so." These people left Plimoth, with some traveling north to Portsmouth to fish, process salt for the curing of fish, cut staves for wood barrels, build furniture, cultivate the land and trade furs with the natives.[2] By 1626, David Thomson[3] and his family had built a trading post at "Panaway"[4] for fishermen and traders, and in 1631, a Great House[5] was built at Strawberry Hill[6] to accommodate the meeting needs for local government, religious services and the storage of arms and ammunition for these early settlers of Portsmouth. The waterfront area was busy with

Pannaway Trading Post, by Coley Cleary. *Author's collection.*

Left: The First New Hampshire Settlers' Monument at Odiorne State Park, Rye, New Hampshire. *Photo by the author.*

Opposite: Abenaki Indians watching as colonists' ships arrive, by Coley Cleary. *Author's collection.*

12

fishermen who would "universally squander their shares, which amounted to (7 to 8 pounds) a man for a voyage of several weeks, on brandy, rum, wine, and tobacco." The few Puritan settlers amongst them congregated away from the shoreline and into the area north of the Mill Pond, calling it "Christian Shore."

The 170 or so Portsmouth-area settlers found Native Americans living in suitable and healthy societies, but they felt the Indians' way of life was inferior to their own. These (Algonquin) Abenaki Indians greatly outnumbered[7] the early settlers, and this, combined with their different way of life, caused fear and drew the suspicion of the settlers. The English showed little respect toward the Indians and soon found themselves battling not just disease and starvation but also, on occasion, the various Indian tribes. When the settlers arrived, they brought with them their traditional culture, which included their means of protection and conflict resolution. They did not have police officers to protect them, but they did bring weapons such as flintlock long guns and matchlock muskets, along with some swords. These weapons were vital necessities not only in helping them with protection but also for hunting food to eat and furs for clothing. Each person (or family) was responsible for his own individual security, but it didn't take long for the settlers to appreciate the value of the group as a force multiplier and to continue the community they had developed while aboard ship. These early community rules included the common shared defense of neighbors.

The Indians and settlers were mostly at peace with one another. Both groups quietly shared the nearby woods for hunting and waters for fishing and frequently traded pelts and other items. In 1628, the Indians apparently had their first guns sold to them by Thomas Morton of Braintree, Massachusetts. Morton had a terrible reputation as the leader of criminals who would sell anything—including liquor, guns and ammunition—to anyone for the right price. This early "mob boss" reveled in loose morals and shocked the nearby Pilgrims in Plimouth so much that they sent Captain Miles Standish to arrest Morton and send him back to England.

Portsmouth was incorporated as "Strawbery Banke" in 1631,[8] and the fragile peace between the Indians and settlers eroded. Soon, Indian hostilities mounted, with frequent attacks and skirmishes. The infant communities at Dover and Portsmouth concluded that they would be too weak to defend against sustained Indian attacks. They also feared legal challenges to their land claims from the Mason family and, in 1641,

Trading, by Coley Cleary. *Author's collection.*

petitioned the government of Massachusetts to place the whole region under its jurisdiction and protection.[9]

With protection and control approved by the government of Massachusetts, the area gained a county court and two deputies when Norfolk County was formed to include Salisbury, Hampton, Haverhill, Exeter, Dover and Portsmouth. Dover and Portsmouth retained their district court to take care of the more local issues such as lying, idleness,

Captain John Smith (of Pocahontas fame), early explorer of the Portsmouth area. *Image the property of the Portsmouth Athenaeum, used with permission.*

drunkenness and "general bad behavior" (i.e., playing shuffleboard or cards). These crimes were punishable by fines that were aimed at keeping servants, slaves and youth in line. More severe crimes, such as petty theft, nonobservance of the Sunday travel ban, evading mandatory observance of the Sabbath by not attending religious services and resting from work during the week, were punished in public with whipping at the town

Early 1600s map of New England, by Coley Cleary. *Author's collection.*

pump[10] or by having one's hands and head placed in a wooden pillory that was housed at the south meetinghouse or, later, in the Parade at the town pump in present-day Market Square. Banishment, or being forced to leave the community, was also a punishment used mostly for heresy.[11] The most serious crimes of murder, rape, adultery, concealing the death of a newborn and being a witch were dealt with by hanging.[12]

PIRATES

Dixy Bull arrived in Boston ready to trade with the Indians. He was a shallop ship's[13] captain and a merchant from London looking to make his fortune buying and selling beaver pelts, but he soon turned into Portsmouth's first fugitive. The year was 1623, and Portsmouth was being settled. Dixy was in the Penobscot Bay area of Maine with a full load of beaver pelts and other trading goods when he became the victim of French pirating and was left with nothing. He returned to Boston, recruited a crew of fifteen men and began exacting his revenge by becoming a pirate preying on the coastal people in and around the foggy Isle of Shoals.[14]

The "dread pirate" plundered from peaceful settlers, stealing jewelry, crystal and silver. When in 1632 he looted the fort and captured several boats in the Pemaquid area of Maine,[15] the townspeople of Portsmouth

Shallop ship, by Coley Cleary. *Author's collection.*

Pirate Dixy Bull, by Coley Cleary. *Author's collection.*

responded by gathering up forty men to pursue Bull, who was escaping eastward. Outfitting four pinnacles[16] and shallops, these men could be called our first law enforcement officers as they fearlessly pursued this fugitive in what might be considered the police cruisers of their day. Suddenly, a storm arose, and the small fleet of colonists was scattered, allowing Bull to escape. The legend of the pirate Dixy Bull did not end here, though. The fate of the first recorded pirate in New England waters is not certain, but many believe that "God destroyed this wretched man." In other words, he was hanged for his crimes when he was later captured in England.

CONSTABLES

The selectmen needed people to help carry out the day-to-day business of the community and appointed the first constables in 1652 to "collect fines and taxes, to keep order at meetings and on town thoroughfares, and to fine and if need be, run out of town, those without a respected last name, and ne'er-do-wells." These selectmen chose as constables Mr. Briant Pendilton, John Pickringe, Renald Fernald, Henry Sherbon and James Johnson, and they

> *shall have full Power to—and lay out, land according as they thinke Beste for the conueininsy and the Towne: Ane wee fully agree, that theas be-for named Towns men shall have full power, to order all our Towne affayrs, as though our selves the wholl Towne wear Presents…to call into question or Fine anny mane in case of—or breach of order.*

This record shows that men were formally selected to keep order, similar to modern police officers, but clearly as a responsibility secondary to their duties in resolving land disputes.

In a process that was called "warning out," these first constables were responsible for challenging loiterers or strangers to post cash bonds to prove they had the means to support themselves and their families. One example was in October 1671, when Mr. Shipway and Henry Dering were named constables, with Dering given a warrant to remove Mr. Henry Russel from the town unless "he Doth give the Towne good Security to beare and Keepe the Towne harmless from being burthened in way of Chrge." Another documented case was in 1692, when Roger Thomas was forced to leave town when he could not produce the demanded security deposit.

Other examples include a July 20, 1686 incident in which the families of John Kelley, Peter Harvie, John Reed and Mis Stocker were summoned by the constables to attend the selectmen's meeting to explain why they had strangers in their homes without the selectmen's permission. John Kelley explained that they were his wife and two children, and he was made to give bond for them, which he promised within the week. Peter Harvie said his guests were his sister and her two children, and he was made to promise to give security as well. There is no written explanation for the cases of Reed and Mis Stocker, but it was written in the selectmen's record that they agreed to post a security. Also at this hearing, the constables were told to warn Thomas French's and Nicho Hodgon's wives that they had been in town too long without permission. Goode Chasely was given "but a fortnight from this day" to leave town, "being no inhabitant."[17] One month later, on August 27, 1686, Peter Harvie did not post his promised bond and was ordered to remove his sister and her two children from his house and return them to Boston, from "whence shee came or otherwise to be convaied by the constables from Town to Town till she com their."

Those who would not or could not post this bond were deemed to be unwilling or unable to be productive citizens of the community and were run out of town. What brought these orders from the selectmen might be

An early settler banished from the community, by Coley Cleary. *Author's collection.*

traced to the fact that there were few jobs, and the town had little means to support those who could not support themselves against famine, smallpox[18] or Indian attack. Warning out protected the limited resources of the young Portsmouth community for those who were able to enhance or at least replace community capital, but the constables lacked a criminal justice system with which to formally arrest and deal with those who refused the order to leave.[19] The few who defiantly remained were shunned with communal peer pressure and were denied a public voice in government or a share in any collective bounty or public assets.

To honor founder John Mason, who in 1634 was captain of the Port of Portsmouth in Southeast Hampshire, England,[20] the area, in 1653, was named Portsmouth because of its resemblance to a good English shipping harbor, its importance to trade and "it being the river's mouth."[21] Indians abounded, as was evident in the naming of Sagamore Creek after the early settlers found the chieftain,[22] or sagamore, of an Indian tribe living on its banks. The area was "alive with hostile red-men" with the "sturdy pilgrim…sleeping with his firelock at his bedside, not knowing at what moment he might be awakened by the glare of his burning hayricks and the piercing war-whoop." New Hampshire had as many as twelve different Indian tribes such as the Nashua, Souhegan, Merrimack, Ossipee and Winnipiseogee. Many locations, such as Exeter, Dover and Manchester, rejected the names of the Indian tribes living there and renamed these areas during the next one hundred years after the English towns that they closely resembled.

Early laws were shaped heavily around a mix of Anglican (Church of England or the Episcopal Church) and Puritan religious beliefs, enforced with an English common legal system.[23] But most who would settle the area did so not so much for religious reasons but because of fishing and trading. Even those who came for religious reasons differed in their religious values. Some settlers believed that a life lived pure, with no vice, no sin and extreme amounts of work, would be rewarded upon death with everlasting existence in heaven, while others were more aligned with Calvinism, which regards as one of its five "doctrines of grace" the notion of predestination. Portsmouth was more aligned with those believing that good works and strict compliance with Bible teachings would lead to heaven.

Crime was considered a form of sin that threatened the immortality of moral and righteous people. Life was important, but greater was the hereafter for those who lived their lives in conformity to strict rules. The selectmen aligned local government with religious beliefs so much that they even included these beliefs in the official town records, as exemplified in the following passage from the 1645 official town records:

> *If you will End your work in peace*
> *Then secke to God: and Doe not feare*
> *To Gide you all from first to last*
> *Till good thereof you all Doe last.*

Rules to be followed governing things like murder and stealing were referenced in the Bible, while things like having long hair, flirting, card playing and drinking alcohol were considered to be "lures by the Devil" and needed strict controls. Sin was a crime and crime was sin, with many laws quoting church preaching or biblical passages. The people maintained a close watch over one another, alerting one another or reporting heathens to the justice of the peace, who would hear cases in a courtroom setting, often in his own home.

On March 27, 1654, Portsmouth selectmen noted that "1 John Jackson and [George Walton erased] Mr Bacheler are chosen constabulis[24] for the next year inseuing." The town was divided into two districts (Great Island and Strawbery Banke),[25] and the constables were responsible for the oversight of their districts. They were paid a modest amount of money for the time, and the responsibility of constable was civic duty, not meant to replace their existing professions. Most served for one year, until the next year's election, when others would be chosen. This system of selecting people to serve as constables continued until 1850, when the police department was formed and the position of police officer became a paid full-time profession. Those who were selected and refused to serve paid a fine in exchange for duty. These constables, working later with the tithingmen, were responsible for policing the community, handling drunks, thieves, loiterers, adulterers, robbers, card players, counterfeiters, murderers, pirates and prostitutes, as well as collecting taxes. An example of the constable's responsibility for collecting taxes can be found written in the March 2, 1657 town record: "This day the selectmen have issued out a rate amounting to 78L-14S-02D:[26] to bee gathered in betweene this Day and the tenth of Aprill 58 by the constables of the towne and delivered to the treasurer Capt. Brian Pendlton."

WITCHES AND TITHINGMEN

Goodwife Jane Walford of Portsmouth was accused of witchcraft in April 1656 after Susannah Trimmings blamed her for "placing" a fire in her back and other illnesses. Thirty-five years before the famous Salem witch trials, Goodwife Walford was brought before the court in Dover. Testimony would be given of her strange appearances and odd behaviors.

The story goes that when Walford asked Trimmings for "a pound of cotton," Trimmings refused, stating that she did not have any to spare. Walford then threatened Trimmings, telling her she would be going on a "great journey," and with that, Walford allegedly changed into the shape of a cat and left. Shortly after the warning, Trimmings was struck down with back problems—which she called "a clap of fire on the back" and which she blamed on Walford. Walford was also known to dress in many colors, often wearing a "black hat" on her head, a "red" petticoat and an old green apron.

Trimmings's husband testified that when Trimmings came home on the night Walford "cursed" her, she did so in a "sad condition" and would not speak. He stated that when his wife arrived,

> she passed by me with her child in her arms, laid the child on the bed, sat down on the chest, and leaned upon her elbow. Three times I asked her how she did. She could not speak. I took her in my arms, and held her up, and repeated the question. She forced breath, and something stopped in her throat, as if it would have stopped her breath. I unlaced her clothes, and soon she spake, and said, "Lord have mercy upon me,

*this wicked woman will kill me." I asked her what woman. She said
Goodwife Walford.*

The local doctor testified that while Trimmings appeared healthy, she had trouble speaking and complained of her lower half being numb and without feeling. A neighbor told a story of a visit from a cat believed to be Walford. The cat entered the garden and would not leave. When the owner tried to shoot the cat, the gun misfired, and the cat was soon joined by two others before fleeing the area. What aided the suspicions of witchery was the fact that the gun could not be repaired afterward. Lastly, Nicholas Rowe told of a visit by Walford on two nights when he was asleep during which she placed her hand on his chest and he could not speak. The next day, he experienced great pain. Walford would be acquitted, but she and her husband would spend the next decades answering to the label of witch.[27]

Portsmouth had about fifty or sixty families in 1658 when there was a great earthquake that shook the area. Punishment for crimes included a five-shilling fine for each tree cut or for each load of wood carted away from the town common grounds that was not needed for fencing or firewood,[28] and the excessive drinking of "Kill Devil"[29] was met with a fine of three shillings,[30] four pence,[31] as James Keat found out when he was caught drunk and broke Rachel Webster's sign and door. Rachel was also fined five shillings for keeping "bad order" of her house.[32] Shoemaker Thomas Parker was arrested and given the choice of paying five pounds or taking fifteen lashes for using "aprobrious [sic] and scandalous words" with preacher Joshua Moodley, "a mighty man of gospel [who] labored vigorously in Strawbery Banke." For being drunk, Parker was ordered to pay five shillings or sit "in ye stocks 1 hours [sic] when the Court please."[33]

To aid in punishment, the selectmen's records of September 25, 1662, showed that "a Cage be made or some other meanes Invented by the selectmen to punnish such as sleepe or take tobacco on the Lords Daye out of the meeting or the time of the Publique Exercise."[34] It would take another nine years before this cage was constructed[35] by Captain John Pickering, who was hired by the town to build it near the "west end of the meeting house."[36] The small, exposed jail cell was described as being twelve feet square and seven feet high, with "a good Strng Dore, and to make a Substantiall payre of stocks, and place the same in the said Kage, and also to build upon the rough of the said Kage a firme Pillery, all which Kage, stocks and Pillery is to be built and raised some Convenien space from the Westward end of the meetig house." The studs were ordered to be six inches broad and four

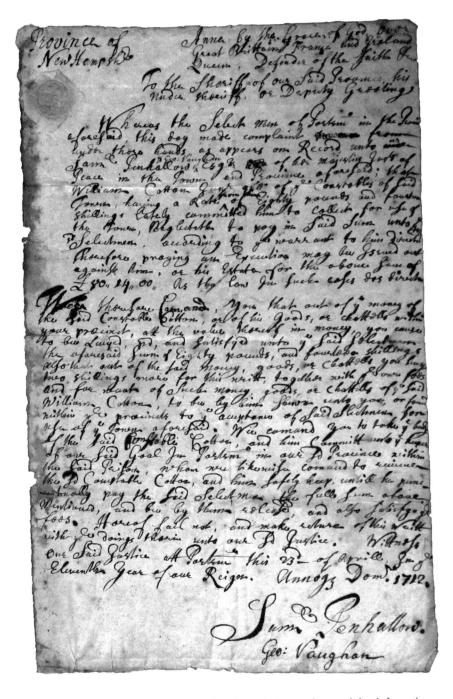

Summons for William Cotton for cutting down timber on the town's land. *Image the property of the Portsmouth Athenaeum, used with permission.*

inches thick, and the openings between them were to be three inches. Those studs on the roof and floor were to be rounded, with construction to be completed by October.

Some of the constables were being replaced because of sickness or resignations, and all citizens were offered five pounds for every wolf they killed within the bounds of the town.[37] The constables of Hampton and Dover were notified in 1662 to be on the lookout for three vagabond Quakers named Amy Tompkins, Anna Colman and Alice Ambrose. Richard Jackson, a woodworker, farmer and mariner, would build his wood-plank and frame house on his family's twenty-five-acre farm in 1664. This house still stands today and serves as New Hampshire's oldest-surviving wood structure.[38] The commissioners sent to America by King Charles II reported back that the "Piscataqua…is a very good harbor, always free from ice and very capable of fortification; and here dry docks might be made."

By 1666, the courts had been firmly established in Portsmouth and Dover. A seven-magistrate panel heard civil and criminal cases, as well as exercised its broad powers by licensing taverns to sell beer[39] and appointing militia officers. This court would sentence Elizabeth Phillips to be publicly whipped and then sent out of town when she was found guilty of "cursing…swearing and entertaining loose fellows at unreasonable times in ye night." The year 1666 also brought a town vote that read that in order to improve the fortifications at Fort Point,[40]

> …every dweller and liver in the towne above sixteen years of age, whether householder, children, servants or any other residing in the towne, shall and doe here promise to worke at the same one whole weeke betwixt this and the last day of October next ensuing, and shall appear on such days as they shall have notice given them from time to time until they have accomplished their several sayd weekes worke, and to be allowed out of their subscriptions three shillings per day, and to be at the Fort by seven o'clock in the morning and to give over at six in the evening, to begin on the Great Island and so round by Sandy Beach, and thence through the whole towne.

After years of skirmishes with the Indians, the townspeople of Portsmouth and Indian chief Squando signed a peace treaty in 1678 that allowed the settlers to "return to their habitations and occupy them without molestation, on condition that they should annually pay the Indians one peck of corn for each family." There would be several peace treaties with the Indians affecting Portsmouth, to include a 1699 treaty, a 1703 treaty and a July 11, 1713 treaty that was ratified in Portsmouth by the eastern Indians of Penacook, Amasacontee, Norridgewoc, Saco and the minor tribes in between and the settlers from Portsmouth to Casco, Maine. These fragile peace agreements needed to be revisited time and time again, with new treaties signed in 1717, 1725 and 1726. These treaties required, in part, that the Indians swear allegiance to the king, and this was one of the contributing factors to their fundamental failure. The Indians refused to completely adopt the settlers' ways, especially regarding loyalty to a king. Most of this Indian fighting was in the western outskirts of the local settlements, such as Kittery, York, Oyster River, Dover and Exeter.

To help the constables manage internal community order[41] and collect taxes, the settlers used the "hundred system," along with tithingmen.[42] This Anglo-Saxon form of community control synced neighbors together in groups of one hundred. These groups would be called tithings and the leaders, tithingmen. Every ten tithings would be organized into a "hundred," with the person in charge of this group called the hundredman. This early form of neighborhood watch helped to resolve conflicts and enforce local rules, especially religious canons such as observance of the Sabbath and manifesting a strong work ethic. The tithingmen were responsible for social control, obedience to Sabbath rules,[43] tax collection and rule enforcement within their tithings and were held accountable by the hundredman.[44]

These hundreds were then lumped into shires, with a shire-reeve selected to oversee the shire. The shire-reeve[45] held a very powerful position, answering only to the justice of the peace,[46] and could lawfully obligate the residents to join in a *posse comitatus*,[47] or a group summoned by hue and cry,[48] to help

TABLE 1

run down and catch criminals or repel rebellions. This hue-and-cry system of forming a posse led by a sheriff matured during the next three hundred years and created the footing for the earliest structure of law enforcement in the United States.

The selectmen voted on March 22, 1678, to "appoynt some honest men to Inspect there Neighbors as the law directs, for preventing drunkeness and disorder." The selectmen carried this out on June 3, 1678, when they appointed "tithingmen to Inspect 10 or 12 of theire Neighbors families." These men would keep watch after the good morals of their neighbors, ensure that no one was "seen loitering about the streets while the bells were tolling the good people to meeting [church services]" and help collect taxes. They also added an order that the tithingmen would enforce the prohibition of profanity on the Lord's Day. Perhaps it was a tithingman who brought forward a 1679 neglect complaint against Jno Davis in regards to his treatment of his wife "like to perish." The selectmen ruled that Davis was not caring for his wife's basic food needs, and they both were told to leave the community within the month "for better security" of the town.

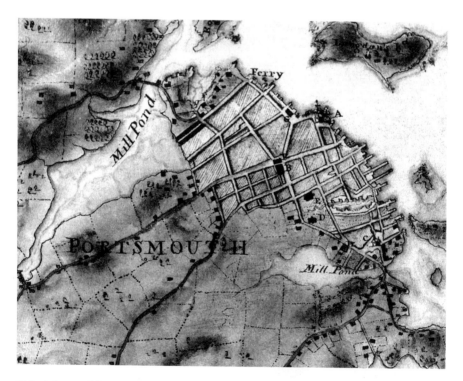

Colonial map of Portsmouth. *Used with permission of William T. and Constance Warren.*

In 1680, New Hampshire was decreed a separate province. John Cutt, Esquire, was appointed president, and Portsmouth was selected as the capital. Fort William and Mary was reinforced and housed eleven cannons for coastal and area defense, and the "demeanor of boys at meetings" must have been troublesome because the town agreed to pay Nicholas Bond twelve shillings a year to "look after" them. Tobias Lakemen, a thin and slight man with graying hair lying underneath his flexible round hat, was in charge of the Portsmouth Jail when his "friendly nature" got the better of him. Some Quakers were sent to jail to await their trial on heresy. On their mere promise to return to court on their trial date, Jailor Lakemen allowed them to leave the jail[49] and go home. The Quakers kept their word and returned for trial, but when Lakemen later extended the same courtesy to a debtor,[50] the debtor never returned, and Lakemen was ordered to pay off the debt. He was also stripped of his job, his property was seized and his family was left penniless.[51] Lakemen tried to earn an honest living but soon became insane. He lived the remainder of his life quite harmless but unable to work. Lakemen would live to be nearly ninety years old, and legend has it that he was never lonely, never hungry and never in want of the things he needed to live because he was never refused at the house of a Quaker or any other person or family he had helped earlier in his life.

CHAOS AND ORDER

Witchcraft and evil spirits continued to be part of the collective superstition of people in the area in 1682. Molly Bridget was a fortuneteller and self-proclaimed witch. She was an inmate in the local almshouse[52] and was thought of as the cause of some of the evils of the day. When hot stones thrown by an invisible hand broke the glass windows of George Walton's tavern, Molly Bridget was thought to be a Lithobolia, or "stone-throwing devil," and the source of this spell.[53] Sometimes there would be strange whistling or the phantom sounds of a trotting horse, and sometimes a boat anchor would suddenly be cast overboard into the water—all without apparent explanation and all blamed on Molly Bridget. When cheese was removed from the press and turned into crumbles on the floor, Molly Bridget would be blamed. When hay bales mowed near the house would blow into the wind and scatter about the home, Molly Bridget would be accused.

It is no wonder, then, that when some pigs got sick, Molly Bridget was blamed. There was an order to remove and burn all the wood chips in the pigsty to kill the wickedness they contained. As the chips burned brightly, Molly could be seen rushing from room to room in a state of frenzy, further proving to the community that Molly was indeed a witch. The tips of the pigs' tails were ordered burned to remove any last signs of wickedness, but the pigs had escaped, never to be found again. As the pigs ran away and the flames subsided, so did Molly's vitality, and when the pigsty fires died, so, too, did Molly Bridget. This, of course, provided the last piece of evidence to prove to the community that Molly Bridget was what she had always claimed to be: a witch.

Twenty colonists were killed and twenty-nine taken captive when Abenaki and Pennacook[54] Indians attacked Dover in 1689. Forty colonists were killed by Indians in 1690 between the Lamprey River in Northwood, New Hampshire, and Amesbury, Massachusetts. An Indian attack on Fox Point[55] left fourteen colonists dead and six captured. A truce shortly afterward calmed hostilities, especially when the Indians returned ten of the captives as a show of good faith, but this peace held for merely six months. In May 1691, a war party of Indians paddled their canoes to Sandy Beach,[56] where they killed or captured twenty-one people, including Captain Sherburne, who lost his life. York, Maine, was surrounded and destroyed by Indians seven months later, in January 1692. Minister Shubael Dummer was one of the first to die in York when he was shot mounting his horse at the door to his house. His wife and family were taken prisoner, and when the fighting was over later that morning, fifty inhabitants lay dead, nearly one hundred were captured and the town had burned to the ground. The people of Portsmouth were summoned to help in the battle, but they arrived too late to "afford relief or retake the captives." By the end of 1693,[57] another truce was in place with the Indians,[58] who desired to be at peace with the English. This truce, though, was more likely caused by the colonists' killing several key Indian leaders in battle and greatly diminishing the Abenakis' ability to effectively fight. The natives again returned English hostages as a sign of good faith.

Great Island seceded[59] and became its own town. Portsmouth shrunk in territory but still included the yet independent portions of Rye and Greenland. Land-hungry settlers pushed the Abenakis farther inland, and the Indians soon realized that they could not live by the conditions agreed upon in the peace treaty. They relinquished their sovereignty and their ability to self-govern. They also agreed to place their trade under English law, which did not allow Indians access to the courts to mitigate disputes. Feeling hopeless, and instigated by the French in Canada, the Indians resumed their attacks on the settlers in 1694.[60] Led by French officer Claude-Sébastien de Villieu, 250 Indians struck Oyster River.[61] When the battle was over, a small group crossed the Piscataqua River under the cover of darkness to widow Ursula Cutt's house.[62] At dawn, and with the sounds of whooping, the war party overran the home, killing Ursula and her three hired hands, who had just begun to mow the fields. The maid escaped and ran to warn the neighbors and seek their help. The Indians anticipated possible neighbor involvement and moved immediately to attack them before they could muster. When the fighting was done later that day, nearly 100[63] people were killed or captured[64] and about twenty buildings were burned. Those who were killed were scalped, with Widow Cutt additionally rumored to have had her ringed fingers[65] severed and taken because the Indians were in a hurry and could not simply slip off the jewelry.

Two years later, during the night of June 25, 1696, the colonists of the Plains[66] were sleeping quietly when fifty Indians from York followed the shoreline in canoes to Sandy Beach. Once ashore, they secretly hiked through the woods off Sagamore Avenue and Peverly Hill Road, taking up positions around the Plains. Just as the sun was about to rise, the settlers awoke early to distinctive war cries and Indians attacking. Five houses were immediately attacked, and fourteen settlers were quickly killed and scalped.[67] Some settlers were able to escape the battle and run downtown[68] to sound the alarm. The colonists quickly mustered and rushed to the Plains. When they arrived, they found the barns and houses ablaze,[69] the dead and wounded scattered about the fields and pathways and the Indians gone, having captured four prisoners. The colonists, led by Captain William Shackford, Lieutenant Libbey and their military company, pursued the attackers throughout the day and into the night. Shortly before daybreak the next day, as the Indians set up for breakfast, the pursuing colonists caught up with this war party five miles away from the Plains. They surprised the Indians, who were unprepared to fight, and the Indians hastily fled, leaving the hostages safely behind. The Indians ran back to Sandy Beach and escaped forever the revenge of their pursuers. The area of the rescue would be called "Breakfast Hill"; today, it is near Route 1 and Breakfast Hill Road in Rye, New Hampshire.

All was not battles and chaos in Portsmouth at the start of the eighteenth century. Portsmouth had about two thousand inhabitants and was the dominant port north of Boston. Businesses were being built downtown, and families were being raised in small wood-frame homes. The first free province school was built for "righters, reeders and Latiners." The town ordered the construction of another jail,[70] this one on the Glebe Lands.[71] Back then, a high sign of civil refinement was the number of successful businesses and schools and increased population growth, along with regulations and laws to follow, with punishments for lawbreakers in the form of gallows,[72] stocks, pillories, torture and jail.

The booming ocean trade had Portsmouth busy building ships, using the nearby forests of straight timber for masts. This wood was also used to produce fine furniture, oars, wagon spokes and barrels. Fishing was abundant, with codfish[73] being the most popular catch, frequently exported to all points of the Atlantic world. In 1671 alone, Portsmouth exported twenty thousand tons of boards, ten thousand quintals[74] of fish, ten shiploads of masts and thousands of furs from the wharfs of the Puddle Dock. Until 1660, there was no customhouse and no inspection of shipping in the port. Thus, smuggler resentment ran high when Deputy Collector Walter Barefoote announced all shipping in and out of Portsmouth would need to be inspected by him. He recorded the major imports during this time as wine, brandy and salt for curing fish.

Portsmouth was the seat of New Hampshire government in 1699, when the New Hampshire Assembly ordered that the first provincial prison[75] be built near Market Square and passed the act that created the first official courts of justice.

Colonial criminal justice generally followed these steps:

- A magistrate was told of a crime by a citizen, constable, tithingman or sheriff.
- If the person had not already been arrested, the magistrate would order the sheriff, marshal or constable to bring the suspect to court.
- The magistrate questioned the accused, often within the magistrate's personal home.
- Lawyers were not involved.[76]
- The magistrate would either dismiss the case or bind the accused over for a trial. Many were allowed to return home while awaiting their trials. Communities were small, so it was difficult for someone to successfully escape, and there were few community resources to care for someone locked up in jail. It was easier and cheaper to allow the accused to be free to work and take care of himself while awaiting trial.
- Trials were set up by the sheriff, who selected jurors and maintained the jails.
- Trials were short, designed to pressure and allow the accused the opportunity to confess and repent. Many people within the community attended these trials because they provided a form of entertainment and drama. Public trials also provided a general deterrence or the chance for the community leaders to reinforce the rules the citizens needed to follow.
- If a confession was given, the magistrate often felt order was restored and issued a lighter sentence, such as twenty-four hours in the stockade or a public whipping. More serious crimes were often met with hanging sentences.[77]

Stockade. *Photo by the author.*

Portsmouth continued to mature. A treaty was signed between England and France that ended almost all hostilities between the colonists and the Indians, several smallpox incidents were being controlled with routine quarantines of sailors and visitors,[78] the town had set aside the area of the Plains for the local militia to drill, the Chase Home for orphaned boys was built[79] and the area had survived several major earthquakes by the time the first recorded murder investigation took place. Abigail Dent was found dead in the swamp near the pasture of George Jaffrey Esquire[80] in 1734. The coroner's inquest stated, "She was murdered by being strangled by the menes of some ill disposed person or persons, by laying violent hands on her throat." She was discovered after being reported missing for several days, and while two sailors were arrested for killing her, they were found not guilty and released. Her murder remains unsolved.

INFANTICIDE

Twenty-seven-year-old Sarah Simpson and the Irish servant Penelope Kenny would be the first two people executed in New Hampshire. Long before legalized abortion, women often dealt with unwanted pregnancies by seeking out a doctor or other person who would perform a crude and illegal abortion procedure. Sometimes the woman would die from excessive bleeding or infection. More often, she lacked the means of obtaining the abortion because the community did not have a conspiring person who would operate in secret or the woman did not have the money or means to go to another community that might have someone to perform the abortion. There are numerous colonial records of a woman who would give birth to a child only to be arrested later for the murder of an infant or the concealment of a dead baby. It seemed that some women would hide their nine months of pregnancy, secretly give birth to the baby, kill it and bury it in the hope that no one would find out. There were many reasons to hide a pregnancy in colonial days, including shame, disgrace and the criminal act of having sex out of wedlock. Another reason was rape, which was often minimized from being a crime because of the perceived "flirtatious actions" of the woman involved. Some pregnancies were unwanted because the family could not support the child once it was born.[81]

On the morning of December 27, 1739, Sheriff Thomas Packer[82] took Sarah Simpson to the South Parish.[83] She had just been convicted, along with Penelope Kenny, of the murder of an infant child. Sarah was a widow and was most likely the natural mother of the newborn, while Penelope, as

Drawing of the hanging of Sarah Simpson, by Coley Cleary. *Author's collection.*

the servant girl, was probably the midwife, although records are not clear.[84] Penelope was escorted to church at Queens Chapel,[85] and both were given sermons by their respective reverends. When services ended, they were both escorted through town riding on a carriage to a large tree near the Pound[86] on Middle Road and South Street. Once they arrived, the condemned had ropes tied around their necks with the other ends tied to a large, strong tree branch.[87] Sarah Simpson and Penelope Kenny stood on the back of a horse-driven cart in their finest church clothes,[88] and Sheriff Packer ordered the horse forward, leaving the two women hanging by their necks.[89] They most likely suffered greatly as they swung in the air, slowly strangulating until dead. Both would be unceremoniously buried there in unmarked graves.

The 1750s saw the start of the Industrial Revolution, the Agricultural Revolution and the seeds being sown for the American Revolution. Gas streetlights were being installed downtown,[90] and the four thousand inhabitants were rattled by another earthquake that rocked the area.[91]

Model of the New Hampshire Statehouse when it was located in Market Square. *Photo by the author.*

Daniel Fowle published the first newspaper in New Hampshire from his office at Pleasant, Washington and Howard Streets,[92] and the town bought its first fire pumper. Portsmouth had three churches: the North and South Meetinghouses and the Queen's Chapel; it had a schoolhouse, a pest house and an almshouse for the poor or mentally ill, and the statehouse was built.[93] Bow and Market Streets[94] were the primary marketplace, and the settlers continued their fragile peace with the Indians.

There even appeared to be some equality and respect given to the Indians, as exhibited when Anthony Bowen and John Morrill were arrested for the peacetime killing of two Indians named Sabatis and Plausawa in Contoocook, New Hampshire.[95] In what years before would have been a condoned act of great courage and honor, these men were now being arrested, indicted, arraigned and held in the Glebe land jail in Portsmouth to await their trial. Not all the colonists agreed with having "white men" answer for the killing of the inferior "red men," so on the eve of their trial, a party of men from Canterbury and Contoocook rode into Portsmouth and took axes to the doors of the jail, releasing Bowen and Morrill. Governor Benning Wentworth[96] was infuriated and instructed the sheriff to arrest all those who had participated in the escape; further, he offered £200 for their capture. While many were later identified as being conspirators in the escape, no one was ever arrested or brought to justice. Both Morrill and Bowen were seen one month later openly working in Canterbury, with no one doing anything to recapture them. In the end, Governor Wentworth calmed his anger and released the pressure to have Morrill and Bowen rearrested. Governor Shirley of Massachusetts advised Governor Wentworth to put the matter aside and to give presents to the families of the Indians as reparations. Governor Wentworth did concede, but it is not known if he gave presents or if other reparations were made. Morrill and Bowen would live out their lives thought of as heroes by most.

The community had other incidents needing investigation. One example was the death of a drunken sailor in 1756. This death was later ruled an accidental drowning when it was determined that the deceased had been fighting with another drunk sailor, with both falling overboard from their docked ship. Another incident involved lawbreakers John Carson and his wife, Margaret, who were both charged and convicted of twenty thefts. John received twenty lashes, while Margaret was fined five pounds and ordered to work as a servant for thirty-three months. Still another investigation involved the burglary of Daniel Jackson's shop in 1750, when twenty-six yards of cloth were stolen. Portsmouth was growing, and the crime associated with this growth also increased.

Laws were enacted to help keep order, with many regulations focused on the excessive consumption of alcohol, which to this day is a root cause for some people committing crimes. It was probably the constables or tithingmen who were charged with posting the names, in 1719, of "drunkards, or common tiplers" as a punishment designed to deter and embarrass others from becoming drunk. This temperate act, along with the banning of Guy Fawkes Day[97] in 1768, was designed to keep the future Americans sober, orderly and of good morals. Those celebrating Guy Fawkes Day faced two days in jail. A drafter of the Guy Fawkes Day ban wrote:

> *It Often Happens that many Disorders and Disturbances are Occasioned and Committed by Loose Idle People under a Notion and Pretence of Celebrating and keeping a Memorial of the Deliverance from the Gunpowder Plot on the fifth of November and the Evening following as Servants and boys Tempted to Excessive Drinking and Quarreling—Surrounding Peoples doors with Clamor and rudely Demanding money of Liquor making mock Shows of the Pope and other Exhibitions making bonfires whereby buildings are in Danger and Populous places and Stealing Materials for such fire with many other Irregularities which Disturb the Pease of Such places and tend to much Corrupt the Manners of Youth.*

Halfway across the world in London, England, a major social reform in policing was about to develop that advocated professional police forces. London was plagued with gangs of "street-robbers" who "committed such daring robberies, and at a time such barbarities, by cutting and wounding those they robbed, in every part of the Metropolis, as spread a general alarm through the Town." English magistrate Sir John Fielding advocated in 1749 for a professional police force called the Bow Street Runners.[98] He argued that in order to reduce crime, the community would need to have professionally trained and paid police officers, ready to respond to crimes and headquartered in a downtown London building on Bow Street. They would be paid £100 for each criminal they arrested. He also valued preventative patrols[99] that became part of the Bow Street Runners' duties. Numbering just six men when the force was started, these forerunners to the "Bobbies" of the Metropolitan Police would number into the hundreds and would last until 1839. They wore red waistcoats and badges as crude uniforms and carried short maces (clubs) with metal receptacles for holding rolled-up arrest warrants (bills)[100] and thirteen-inch-long truncheons with "Bow Street" inscribed on them.

Portsmouth continued with constables, tithingmen and sheriffs upholding its criminal justice system. Eliphaz Dow of Hampton Falls was hanged on May 8, 1755, for the murder of Peter Clough. Dow was the first man executed in New Hampshire. Sheriff Packer once again managed the hanging, this time ordered by Superior Court judge Meshech Weare, who declared, "He [Dow] should be hanged by the neck until he should be dead." The murder occurred on December 12, 1754, when, at the home of Noah Dow (brother of Eliphaz Dow),[101] angry words were exchanged between Eliphaz Dow and Peter Clough. They had been at odds with each other for a long time when they met at this house quite by accident. What was not accidental was Dow picking up his brother's hoe in anger and smashing it into Clough's head, instantly killing Clough. What had started as a chance encounter quickly led to a verbal argument and ended with Clough's death. Dow's hanging was scheduled for three months later, on March 20, 1755, but two governor's reprieves to review Dow's self-defense argument postponed it until May 8, 1755. Between high noon and three o'clock in the afternoon, with many townspeople in attendance, Dow was hanged at the same spot[102] where Sarah Simpson and Penelope Kenny had met their maker sixteen years earlier. After three hours suspended at the end of Sheriff Packer's hangman's rope, Dow was cut down and buried about seventy-five feet away, "on the slope of a small hill." About a century later, skeletal remains excavated by some workers were believed to be Dow's.

The Glebe land jail that was built in 1699 was in need of repair in 1755, but the decision was made to replace it with a new jail, this one built in 1759 at Chestnut Street and Fetter Lane.[103] This area of Chestnut Street would become known as Prison Lane. The jail was described as being "made with square hewed timbers, lined on the inside with solid plank, and covered with iron bars, well spiked to the timber, and lined with plank. It had a dwelling house annexed to it; the whole was two stories high."[104] This oak timber jail would burn down in 1781, when fire spread from the nearby Woodbury Langdon House[105] and Treadwell Barn[106] great fire. A guardhouse was built in 1761 on the hill near the north meetinghouse. A ten-foot-square room set therein would serve the constables as an early police station.

On the cold Friday of January 27, 1764, a woman was caught shoplifting a pair of children's shoes she had hidden underneath her hooded cloak. Someone saw her and told the store owner, who chased after her, yelling, "Thief! Stop, thief!" as she fled the shop on King Street. Goodman Newmarch, a neighbor, heard the commotion and chased down the woman, bringing her to the Honorable Hunking Wentworth, justice of the peace. The shoes were removed, with Justice Wentworth immediately ordering that the woman be publicly whipped at the town pump.[107] Sheriff Packer took custody of her and brought her to the town pump, where he tied her hands and bared her shoulders so he could apply the cat o' nine tails to her bare skin. The local newspaper covered this whipping, writing:

> *Last Friday one of our local female pilferers received a flagellation at the whipping post, which had a great number of spectators to see this good work performed; and it is hoped that others, who so justly deserve it, will soon be brought to the same place to receive their deserts. A Course of Thieving is a direct Road to the Gallows, tho' commonly attended either by Way of the Whipping-Post and Pillory…There is scarcely a Crime so mean, unnatural and disgraceful as Thieving—when once detected, they become the Contempt of Society, and forever after are branded with the odious but true Proverb* [once a thief, always…].

Later that same year, a hostler[108] who stole a bucketful of West India rum from his boss was sentenced to ten lashes of the cat o' nine tails upon his bare back, to be applied at the town pump.

The stage to Portsmouth from Boston was three dollars, and perhaps that was how Benjamin Franklin arrived in 1763. The exact date of his arrival is not known, so maybe he witnessed the chase of the shoe shoplifter or the whippings at the town pump, but that was not what brought him to town. Dr. Franklin's visit was to supervise the Warner House installation of the first lightning rod in New Hampshire. He left town when he was done and avoided the smallpox epidemic of 1764 that was blamed on travelers bringing the highly infectious disease into town with them. The town ordered that gates be built on each road leading into town[109] and manned by armed guards[110] to ensure that all travelers first cleansed themselves in a smokehouse before being allowed passage.

The sheriff and constables must have been present in 1765 when Portsmouth revolted against the Stamp Act,[111] which imposed a direct tax on the colonies to be paid to England. This tax met with great resistance from the people, and the pressure further increased toward revolution. The townspeople formed a mob and chanted, "Liberty, property and no stamps!" as they gathered to attend a mock funeral for the Goddess Liberty on November 1, 1765. Stamp agent George Meserve, Lord Bute and the devil were hanged together in effigy in Haymarket Square.[112]

Portsmouth had 187 slaves[113] in 1767, when Market Street was called Paved Street because it had just become the first street in Portsmouth to

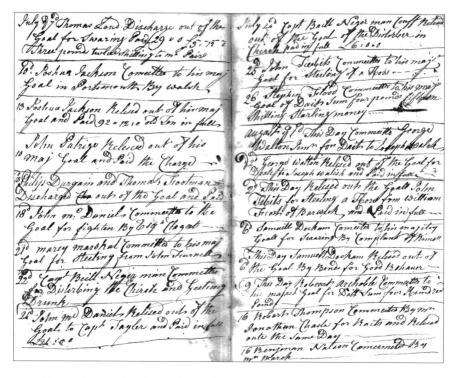

A 1770 jail log. *Property of the Portsmouth Police Department, scanned by the author and used with permision.*

be covered with bumpy cobblestone pavers. The Portsmouth slaves were allowed to form their own mini government, to include a king and a sheriff and to hold trials for some crimes involving slaves. One such case went like this: Prince Jackson was a slave to Nathaniel Jackson of Christian Shore and was accused of stealing an axe. He was brought to King Nero,[114] the leader of the slaves, to "sit for examination." The evidence was presented, and Prince Jackson was found guilty and sentenced to twenty lashes across his bare back. Many slaves attended the whipping, which was at the town pump. Prince Jackson was tied up, his bare back exposed, and just before the first lash was applied, the slave Deputy Sheriff Pharaoh Shores addressed the group, calling out, "Gemmen, this way we s'port our government!" Prince Jackson was released from custody following the whipping, with the order to stay away from Christian Shore unless under the direction of his master or face another twenty lashes.[115]

HANGINGS AND AN
UNSOLVED MURDER

Few things other than the Revolution and the issues leading up to the revolt drew so much government controversy as the hanging of Ruth Blay of South Hampton. There were six hundred crimes punishable by death in 1768, including infanticide,[116] the one that a beautiful, well-educated thirty-one-year-old named Ruth Blay would be found guilty of committing. Court proceedings had begun months earlier, when she was indicted for the killing of her bastard child. The trial on November 24, 1768, affirmed the indictment, with the court handing down the death sentence in the form of a public hanging. It started in the fall of 1767, when the schoolteacher and seamstress from Hawke, New Hampshire,[117] became pregnant out of wedlock. She was able to hide the fact that she was pregnant from her family and neighbors by wearing very bulky dresses, which were fashionable in those days. Strong rumors suggested that the father was the local preacher, but the truth will never be known, as neither Blay nor any known records revealed the father's name.

In the spring of 1768, the pregnant Blay moved to South Hampton, New Hampshire, and on her birthday, June 10, she gave birth to a baby girl. Blay would explain that the baby was stillborn, but there were no witnesses to confirm this because she was alone when she gave birth. In what would be the most damaging fact of the case for Blay, she hid the lifeless body in the loose floorboards of the neighboring Clough family barn. A law of 1759 titled "An Act to Prevent the Destroying and Murdering of Bastard Children" addressed any claim of stillborn children and the act of concealing their death in this manner:

...If any woman be delivered of any issue of her body, male or female, which if it were born alive should be a bastard, and they endeavor privately, either by drowning, or secretly burying thereof, that it may not come to light, whether it was born alive or not, but be concealed; in every such case the mother so offending shall suffer death, as in the case of murder.

Four days later, some children were playing in the barn and discovered the body of the infant. The constable of South Hampton was Isaac Brown, and he arrested Blay based on a warrant from the provincial justice of the peace, Philip White. A jury of sixteen men was formed as a coroner's inquest to determine the cause of death. Later in the day on June 14, 1768, they all agreed that the child was not stillborn but "came to its death by violence."

As was the practice in colonial days, prisoners were often kept in the homes of the local constable until they could be transported to a jail. On June 18, Blay was ordered transported from Constable Brown's house to the provincial jail in Portsmouth, but she was very ill from the effects of the unattended childbirth and was instead confined for the next thirty-five days at the home of Benjamin Clough. On a warm July 19, after having completely recovered,[118] Ruth Blay was brought to the jail on Prison Lane[119] by Constable Brown. On August 2, 1768, she was brought to the court, which was located on the west end of the old province's Assembly House,[120] across from the North Church on King Street. She pleaded not guilty. The trial of *King v. Blay* thus began on September 21, 1768, and was over that afternoon. Early the next day, the twelve-man jury handed down a guilty verdict. The local *New Hampshire Gazette and Historical Chronicle* newspaper reported on Friday, September 23, 1768:

Wednesday last at His Majesty's Superior Court of Judicature...Ruth Blay of South-Hampton...of about 25 [sic] years of Age, was tried for Murder of her Bastard Child and found Guilty—The Trial lasted from Ten o'Clock, A.M. to Six in the Afternoon, and the Jury were out almost the whole Night before they were agreed, and Yesterday Morning brought in their Verdict.

Blay was condemned to be hanged by her neck until dead, with the execution date set for November 24, 1768. Ruth would be granted three death sentence reprieves by Governor John Wentworth, all for the same reason: to better prepare herself to face death. His third and final reprieve clearly stated that the sentence was to be carried out on December 30, 1768, between the hours of ten and two o'clock. The evening before the hanging, she gave "her DECLARATION and CONFESSION which she sign'd in Presence of three Witnesses, at Eight o'clock in the Evening…& stood by to the last, as told by the Printers." The next morning, Sheriff Packard called for the noose to be prepared at Gallows Hill[121] and delivered a shrieking Blay for a high-noon hanging on a day that had freezing rain falling over a light coat of snow. One thousand spectators attended, and Sheriff Packard was asked to hold off until the very last minute while the condemned's friends attempted to gain another reprieve or perhaps a full pardon. Sheriff Packard was heard to have stated that he did not want to be late for his dinner (lunch), and the sentence was hurriedly carried out.

Galloping horse's hooves could be heard approaching from the distance minutes after Blay had slowly strangled to death hanging at the end of the rope tied to the extended tree branch. A mere ten minutes after her white silk– and satin-clothed body was hanged, a rider arrived and presented to Sheriff Packard a pardon from the governor—but alas, it was too late. Ruth Blay was dead. Sheriff Packard then unceremoniously buried her in an unmarked grave near Gallows Hill and went to his house for dinner. Later that evening, the townspeople gathered at his house[122] and hanged him in effigy, with a sign reading, "Am I to lose my dinner, this woman for to hang? Come draw away the cart, my boys, don't stop to say Amen."

Although there are many references to parts of Ruth Blay's story that include the tragic timing and thin reasoning behind Sheriff Packard's order, along with the governor's pardon arriving mere minutes too late to save Ruth Blay, researcher/author Carolyn Marvin is quick to point out that although she, too, retells much the same story, she could not find independent primary sources to corroborate the last pardon or the sheriff being burned in effigy the night Ruth Blay was hanged. I, too, could not find any independent news accounts to validate the story that Sheriff Packard rushed Blay's hanging so he would not be late for dinner, nor is there any mention in the local newspaper or the governor's records of Ruth Blay receiving a pardon or Sheriff Packard being hanged in effigy. Sheriff Packard was replaced two years later, in 1770, by John Parker and died a rich man the following year, in 1771.

New Hampshire was divided into five counties, with Sheriff Parker being the first sheriff of Rockingham County. Portsmouth had ordered that there be at least three constables selected at all times, but the majority of law enforcement and criminal investigations continued to fall to the county sheriff. The larger cities of Boston, New York and Philadelphia were using constables for all-purpose police protection and criminal investigations. Portsmouth, however, was limiting constables and night watchmen to basic crime prevention and civil rule enforcement while the sheriff was responsible for arresting criminal suspects, jailing prisoners and carrying out punishments, including executions.

Simply put, the sheriff was tasked with more serious crimes that today would be considered felonies, while the constables had the more minor violations and misdemeanors.[123] Crimes such as preventing youth from attending "theatrical performances" because "they expose our youth to many temptations and youthful lusts" would be left to the constable and judge to enforce, while serious theft, murder and sex crimes would be handled by the sheriff, who worked mostly out of his house or the provincial jail. The Portsmouth constables and night watchmen were loosely formed under the selectmen, and many had other jobs such as storekeepers and blacksmiths. These "watchers" would take turns patrolling the streets for dangers, fires, Indians and the bad conduct of others. The constables also worked mostly out of their homes or businesses because there was no physical police station or sheriff's building in the colonial days of Portsmouth.

Crimes during the Revolutionary War period were either limited or largely unrecorded. The theft of two bags of money that contained £160 from the house of Samuel Penhallow and the burglary of Mr. Cutt's dry goods store[124] are notable events to showcase that Portsmouth was not crime-free. There were also more serious crimes, such as the unsolved murder of French sailor John Dustin in the area of Creek or present-day Frenchman's Lane;[125] however, the newspapers and other documents that have survived focus on the exploits of the taking of Fort William and Mary in New Castle,[126] the ride of Paul Revere to downtown Portsmouth[127] or the reading of the Declaration of Independence by Sheriff John Parker from the balcony of the statehouse on Congress Street.[128] Just a few decades earlier, the colonists had fought off the Indians, and soon this community of 4,590 people[129] would join the fight in a war with a world superpower. It's no wonder much of the community's focus was on debating participation, politics and preparations for war and not on recording crimes and punishment.[130]

A MODEL POLICE FORCE

With the Revolutionary War behind it, the town of Exeter became the state capital,[131] while Portsmouth would further develop its downtown[132] commercial and civil infrastructure.[133] At the turn of the century, shipbuilding, textiles and trade were the predominant industries in Portsmouth. The New Hampshire Bank[134] was established in 1792 as the first bank in the state, and since then, Portsmouth has never been without a bank. French balloonist Francois Blanchard delighted nearly three thousand residents when he conducted aeronautical demonstrations in 1796. VIPs such as President George Washington and the Marquis de Lafayette had visited, and a new jail was built on Islington Street.

This jail was built on June 22, 1782, at the corner of Brewster and Islington Streets and was expanded with a stone addition fifty years later. The first keeper was Ebenezer Chadwick, who ran it until 1800, when Sheriff Timothy Gerrish took over until 1815. Gerrish's son Andrew took command from 1815 until 1835, with George W. Towle manning it until 1856 and, finally, Joseph B. Adams in charge until it closed in 1891. The front yard was used for prisoners sentenced to be lashed, branded or whipped. Many of them were known to have begged for mercy as their bare backs bled onto the ground below. In 1804, a sixty- or seventy-year-old man named Morse was whipped thirty-nine times for counterfeiting. Samuel Hogg was whipped and branded for an unknown crime. In 1806, Nehemiah Clam and John Wilson were whipped for an unknown crime. In 1808, James Brown was also whipped and branded, while in 1810, John Bickford was thought to be the last man branded. This jail was

Portsmouth Islington Street Jail, circa 1880. It was used from 1782 to 1891. *Image the property of the Portsmouth Athenaeum, used with permission.*

used until the Penhallow Street County Jail was built and opened in 1891. The Islington Street Jail was sold on January 23, 1907, and the granite blocks were used for the foundation of a building on Vaughn Street.

There were catastrophic fires[135] that decimated the downtown area, but the city rebuilt each time, gradually increasing the use of fireproof brick rather than wood for construction. Portsmouth was a world leader in shipping cargo, and the Portsmouth Naval Shipyard[136] became the first in the young United States. Even the great Daniel Webster was calling Portsmouth home[137] as he established his first law office on Market Street.

Crime continued, but the offense for which Ruth Blay was hanged was repealed.[138] On September 17, 1800, German-born cooper Frederick H.J. Hein killed his entire family before turning the gun on himself. In one of the earliest recorded murder/suicides in the United States, Hein began his day by killing Charles W. Taylor, a hardware merchant on Market Street, and then walked back home to 8 Islington Street, where he shot and killed his three daughters—Caroline (fourteen), Maud (thirteen) and Bertha (eleven)—before taking his own life.

Portsmouth, like other areas of the world, was trying to improve its system of criminal justice and law enforcement by looking at other models already in place. The Portsmouth constables still existed, but the recognition of a more independent and professional police officer was found in 1800 with the selection of the city's first.[139] The police officer and the constables would be centrally headquartered in the city's new brick market building, called Jefferson Hall, on

Jefferson Hall housed the city's brick market and police department.
Image the property of the Portsmouth Athenaeum, used with permission.

Pleasant Street.[140] Edward Hart was nominated and elected as the first police officer for Portsmouth, but he was not present to accept. A constable was sent for him, and when he arrived, he stated:

> *Mr. Moderator: I have been informed by your messenger, that the town has unanimously elected me Police Officer for the current year. The duties of the office are of the highest importance and responsibility, and it will require much labor and persevering effort to perform its duties to your satisfaction. No one, ten or twenty men can succeed acceptably, if at all, without the cordial co-operation of his good feeling townsmen: but with such aid, much may be effected [sic] even by one man. I will accept the office to which the town has elected me, and perform its duties according to the best of my abilities, upon one condition. That condition is, that in discharging my duties all my good fellow townsmen will lift the helping hand!*

He then lifted his right hand high above his head as if to take an oath and addressed the crowd: "Mr. Moderator, with this assurance of the co-operation of my fellow-townsmen so unanimously expressed, I accept of the office, and am ready to be qualified." This highly respected man then left the room, and within twenty-four hours, everyone in the town knew they had selected Mr. Hart as Portsmouth's first police officer and that he was called to be the one "sent for the punishment of evil doers and for the praise of them that do well."

Officer Hart and the constables addressed similar issues to those seen all over the civilized world. For example, homelessness existed during this time, as exemplified by the "hermit of Sagamore['s]" death in 1820 after "living a solitary and lazy life" in the woods around Sagamore Creek. The barn of the great Nathaniel Adams was burned down by a suspected serial arsonist in 1804, and though a man named Charles Stewart was arrested and tried, he was acquitted. Later, a barn opposite the schoolhouse on School Street, owned by Mr. Perkins Ayers, was the object of a fire that was quickly doused. Located inside was a tin pot that contained the incendiary. A neighbor named Sukey Nutter became an immediate suspect when it was learned that before she moved to the School Street area, she had been living in the Plains at the times of the previous barn fires. She was also heard to say at one time "I'll burn you up" to Captain Chase when he told her that he was going to expose some of her previous bad behaviors. She was arrested but never tried. Instead, she was allowed to leave the area with the promise never to return. When she left, she fell into the company of, and later married, Charles Stewart, who had left Portsmouth months earlier after his arrest and acquittal for the arsons at the Plains.

Weather, too, must have been a problem for Officer Hart and the constables, with some winter storms dropping three feet of snow at one time, causing ten-foot drifts. They must have patrolled the areas of the Public Bathhouse on Cross Street, where any person could get a bath for twenty-five cents or buy a coupon to receive five baths for one dollar.[141] In 1804, men were being whipped and branded[142] at the Islington Street jail for crimes such as counterfeiting.[143] Officer Hart and the constables most likely were involved in investigating these crimes.

The foreign trade embargo that President Thomas Jefferson declared in 1807 brought the Portsmouth economy of shipbuilders, sailors and sail makers to a standstill until the War of 1812 broke out. The police force increased during this depressed economic time to four police officers. They would have walked the first sidewalks laid down in Portsmouth in 1808 and surely would have talked with many of the 6,934 inhabitants in 1810.

In 1811, there was a volunteer police force in place. It was headquartered in the almshouse[144] located on Jaffrey Street.[145] This building, erected in 1755–56, also served as the house of corrections, with William Vaughn serving as its superintendent.[146] These officers would be used to help police the city, as well as being responsible for printing and dispersing parts of the written laws for the citizens to read. Handbills and posters would be printed and posted on street corners, and from time to time, these volunteer police officers would assist the local teachers in explaining the laws to students. Even the ministers were asked to cover a law from time to time during Sunday services. Some of the laws the selectmen wanted wider community understanding of were the banning of fireworks downtown, the five-miles-per-hour downtown speed limit for horses and carriages, the dogs-at-large laws[147] and the rule that licenses were required in order to sell liquor. John F. Robinson challenged the liquor license law by selling grog[148] out of the unlicensed cellar of his store at Spring Market Place at Ceres Street. He was arrested several times, but there was no mention of his fate or punishment.

The police were organized into six patrols (shifts) per day, with unexcused absences from duty being met with a twenty-five-cent fine. By 1818, there would be forty-four policemen patrolling Portsmouth. A possible reason for the increase in police officers might have been the influx of people because of the War of 1812. In 1814, there were five thousand militiamen stationed in Portsmouth to protect it from the British. There were also numerous privateers[149] using Portsmouth as a homeport, and they captured 419 British vessels, selling them and their goods in Portsmouth for over $2.5 million. One ship alone, named the *Fox*, was financed locally and manned by Portsmouth sailors, earning over $500,000 in booty during the war. The local economy boomed during the war because of the privateers, as did the shipyard, which began its long tradition of building U.S. Navy warships when it completed and launched the seventy-four-gun man-of-war USS *Washington* in 1815.

Portsmouth had a model police force in 1816. The governor received petitions from other towns asking for a "police law similar to the Police of Portsmouth." These requests were denied because the governor did not like the fact that a single person with the title of police officer could arrest a citizen without first obtaining a magistrate's approval. A Portsmouth Police officer could arrest without a warrant for offenses such as idleness, profane talk,[150] improper writing on fences or transgressing the rules of good order; this was an unprecedented level of police authority in New Hampshire at the time. In 1817, the town was still using constables. This was also the year that Daniel Webster closed his law practice on Market Street and headed for Boston.

In 1820, the U.S. Naval Shipyard was in demand building warships. Most of the 7,327 inhabitants[151] were involved somehow with the shipyard economy, and to ease Portsmouth's access, the first bridge was built across the Piscataqua connecting Kittery (and the shipyard) with Portsmouth. Portsmouth had established the first Sunday school in the country, the textile factories were producing 300,000 shirts each year and the Rockingham Hotel opened.[152] The area was bustling with progress and its people with pride. Portsmouth had reached sustainable prosperity and security. Nathaniel Adams wrote of Portsmouth at the time:

The air of Portsmouth is salubrious; the inhabitants are generally healthy, and it is not uncommon to find persons between eighty and ninety years

Portsmouth, circa 1830. *Oil on canvas by John Samuel Blunt (1798–1835). Presented to the city on December 18, 1878, by Colonel William H. Sise, mayor. Photo by the author.*

of age; there is one woman living upwards of one hundred and four years of age, in the full enjoyment of her mental faculties, and who was able to walk the last summer between eight and ten miles in a day. There are eight societies for religious worship in Portsmouth; one Episcopal, two Congregational, one Independent, one Baptist, one Methodist, one Universalist, one Sandemanian. Great attention is paid to the education of children. Seven public schools and several private ones, are maintained for their instruction, besides district schools kept by women. The town pays annually nearly five thousand dollars to the instructors. There are seven houses for public worship; one Academy; five school houses in the compact part of the town, and two in the outskirts; a court house, gaol [sic], three markets, and the building belonging to the Athenaeum. This institution is very flourishing. The proprietors purchased the building belonging to the New-Hampshire Fire and Marine Insurance Company, situated on the Parade, and have appropriated the lower story for a reading room, which is furnished with the best newspapers published in the principal cities of the United States. In the second story is the library, containing nearly two thousand volumes, to which additions are annually made. In the upper story is a large collection of natural and artificial curiosities, minerals, coins, etc. The institution is esteemed a great ornament and advantage to the town.

A POLICE DEPARTMENT IS BORN

Being a constable or police officer must have been difficult leading up to the 1850s. There was little known about how to best police people in a community. The men (and they were always men at this point) were selected primarily through a popular election, and there was little or no compensation involved. Most served to avoid being fined by the community, but there were some whose names appear over and over again on documents, suggesting that some men served out of a sense of duty or at least a fondness for the work. There were few written laws and no equipment, uniforms had not yet been introduced and standardization of police practice was just beginning, mostly in Europe, but it would soon spread to America. The time was fast approaching that would compel police systems to evolve with better leadership, management and uniformity.

Communities all over reorganized their local form of government, and within the next twenty years, police departments were being created as official branches of local government. The era of loosely managed policing by night watchmen, military soldiers, elected constables and tithingmen was being replaced with police officers managed in a civilianized structure using deliberately organized bureaucracies. The police would be answerable to the public and not to the military or to any individual alderman. Chicago Police Department was formed in 1837; New York,[153] Boston and Philadelphia Police Departments were formed in 1844; and the San Francisco Police Department was formed in 1849. That same year in Portsmouth, on September 21, 1849, a ballot measure was passed by a 4-vote margin (459–

455) that established Portsmouth, New Hampshire, as a city with a mayor as the chief executive authority effective January 2, 1850.[154] This charter also created the Portsmouth Police as a city department.

Mayor Abner Greenleaf appointed twenty-two men to serve as police watchmen patrolling south to South School House, north to the North Hay Scales, west from Cabot Street to Islington Road and then to the millpond. Andrew J. Beck, a carriage maker by trade living at 82 State Street, was appointed the first city marshal and given a salary of $200 per year. The city marshal had the control and direction of the city police and served at the will of the mayor[155] and aldermen. He was chief constable and police officer. This represented the first time Portsmouth records used the term "city marshal" for the head of the police. The marshal had the authority to arrest and detain; to execute warrants and summonses; to clear city streets, vacant lots and alleys of "nuisances"; and otherwise see to it that all ordinances of the town were observed. The assistant marshals and police constables were paid $50 per annum, and all were required to have with them their city-issued identification badges while on duty. All took oaths of office and were required to post bonds of $300 each to ensure the "faithful performance of the duties of his respective office."

In 1850, the city forbade Sabbath sales of shellfish, cigars, nuts and confectionery of any kind. The stage made three trips a week to Kennebunk, Maine, to deliver people and the mail; the steamer *Portsmouth* was making three trips a week to Boston at a cost of $1.50 per passenger; the population was 9,738; and there were seventeen ships, one bark, three brigs, seventy schooners and one sloop based out of Portsmouth. The fire department had six manual pumpers with two thousand feet of hose, there were four banks in town, the rail line connecting Epping and Portsmouth was completed[156] and the shipbuilding business thrived as sleek, fast clipper ships were being made at Portsmouth's dry docks.[157] The city marshal was required "from time to time to pass through the streets, lanes and alleys of the city and take notice of all the nuisances endangering the health of the city and report same to the health committee."[158]

One reason for a professional and paid police force might have been the public's general sentiment, as exemplified in this 1847 editorial:

> *If you want good order you must sustain the police. Then again, parents are very much in the wrong—you will see every day and particularly on the Sabbath, a gathering of young rowdies, using profane language, making scandalous remarks to, or about everyone that passes by; smoking cigars, etc;*

*ages range from 10 to 16 years and upwards. I ask who will be willing to
serve as police officers under the present circumstances.*

In 1853, City Marshal Jonathan Dearborn complained to the mayor
about rowdy boys and lack of police officers when he wrote, "It is not
uncommon for the police to discover young boys from 13 to 16 years of
age—intoxicated. There is a need for more police officers in addition to
our present numbers." In response, the mayor authorized sixty-four "special
Officers," and the present-day Portsmouth Auxiliary Police was formed.
These officers would work part time and be paid anywhere from one dollar
to eighty dollars per year depending on the amount of time worked. Crimes
reported to the police officers included, in part:

*Riding on the sidewalk; Sabbath breaking; defacing buildings; night
walking; disturbing schools; bathing in public places; brawling; following
ladies; exposing person; profane or obscene language; keeping disorderly
house or house of ill fame; operating billiard tables, bowling alleys or other
forms of gaming without permit; crying "Fire!"; street walking; cruelty
to animals; assaults on wives by husbands; juggling; gambling; throwing
stones; rescuing prisoner* [aiding the escape of a prisoner]; *runaway
boys; violating lobster laws; stealing railroad rides; attempt to ravish; insult,
rude, indecent or disorderly conduct; and giving away liquor.*

In 1853, the City of Concord, New Hampshire Police was formed.[159]
The NYPD required a full police uniform to be worn in addition to the
existing eight-point badge, and it became the first police department in
America whose officers wore complete police uniforms with hats.[160] The
Boston Police had successfully merged both its day and night watches to
become a unified full-time police department, modeling itself closely on the
London Metropolitan system, which adhered to a civilianized professional
non-paramilitary organizational structure.[161] Portsmouth was operating
similarly under the command of the city marshal, who would be frequently
replaced by the mayor. By the time the Civil War broke out in 1865, a total
of ten changes of command at the city marshal's position had taken place.
While larger departments were moving forward in their systems of police
management to include addressing crime and the more efficient deployment
of personnel, the Portsmouth Police were mired with inconsistent leadership.
In fact, it would not be until 1895, when the police commission was formed
and control of the city marshal position was taken away from the mayor, that

the police department began to have longevity and consistency. There were twenty-three city marshals from the year 1850 until 1895, when the police commission took over appointments and control of the city marshal from the mayor. The average tenure of the marshal during this time was 1.9 years. After the establishment of the police commission, the average tenure of the city marshal (or present-day police chief) became 8.5 years. The inconsistency in police command, coupled with the lack of proven police management systems during the mid- to late 1800s, must have made it difficult for the Portsmouth Police Department to address and fix complicated issues such as high crimes, prostitution, gambling, drunkenness and vagrancy.

City Marshal Andrew Beck, in his address to the mayor in 1854, wrote, "In nearly all cases of vagrancy and when persons have been provided with lodging in the watch house, they were roving, lazy, idle and dissipated, without money or any means to procure the necessities of life." City Marshal Oliver Hanscom, just a year later, would write of high crimes and vice in his report, seemingly taking the police department in a different direction of addressing crime rather than just quality of life issues such as vagrancy and drunkenness. Marshal Hanscom would be replaced just a year later, and Marshal Beck was reinstated with the focus again being returned to quality of life issues. Beck highlighted in his 1856 report to the mayor that, under his watch, a decrease in drunkenness arrests had occurred, dropping to only three persons in a thirty-day period, and also underscored the effectiveness of the newly created city agency that monitored the sale of spirituous liquors. The pay the marshal received was also in flux, as was demonstrated when Marshal Hanscom received $350 per year while Marshal Beck, a year later, would receive only $250.

ROGUES AND
QUESTIONABLE CHARACTERS

While police departments today are better trained and the means of investigating crimes better developed, police in the 1850s were quite adept and active at discovering and investigating crime. On a March evening in 1858, a friendly neighbor meeting between the Spinneys of White's Road and Nelson Downing of Dennett Street in Portsmouth would turn deadly for Sarah Spinney. It began when the Spinneys decided to take a walk to visit Nelson Downing of 17 Dennett Street. Soon, Daniel Spinney was arguing with Downing, who was upset that Spinney had helped get Theodore F. Rowe rehired at the navy yard. Rowe previously had been fired, and now Downing was going to be forced to work under Rowe's direction. A fistfight soon broke out, with neither party getting the upper hand in the few blows exchanged. The Spinneys left and began their walk home.

Downing retrieved a gun and told others in the area that he was going "to get Dan Spinney's meat." He then headed toward White's Road, which was about one mile away. Marshal Elisha G. Ferguson was told of the fight and Downing's threat but did nothing to intervene. Meanwhile, Downing quickly snuck to the Spinneys' house, where he hid until the Spinneys returned. As the couple returned home, Sarah reached down to pick up one of her children when a gunshot rang out. She dropped dead from a shotgun blast to her eye, while Daniel was injured in the arm by one of the stray pieces of buckshot.[162] Downing took flight to his friend James Gove, whom Downing forced to house him overnight. The next morning, Marshal Ferguson was in pursuit of Downing after investigating the murder and learning that the suspect might be at his friend's house. Downing was one step ahead of the marshal and his police officers and left the house early the next morning. Downing did not run far but took up hiding in Gove's shed in the back of the house. The police wisely searched the outbuildings before they left Gove's house and found Downing hiding. The police officers placed Downing under arrest. He was later tried, found guilty of manslaughter and sentenced to one year in prison.

While some crime was caused by the local citizens, this was not always the case, as we learn from Mayor Reding, who wrote in 1860 about the problems of visitors: "We are constantly being visited by rogues and questionable characters from other places, and these classes demand not a little attention of our Police." There were 9,335 residents of Portsmouth in 1860, and the 1861 police arrest log showed a total of 1,155 arrests, or roughly 10 percent of the population.[163] The community was either very unlawful and the police perhaps unyielding or Mayor Reding was correct in pointing out the problems with visitors who would not have been counted in the census as residents. Of these arrests, 405 were for public drunkenness; 286 for lodgers; 4 for desertion from the navy; 16 for breaking and entering; 4 for Sabbath Day violations; 10 for escaping from the county jail; 33 for brawls; and 5 for resisting arrest. There were 12 watchmen[164] appointed by the city council, with the city marshal assigned as captain of the watch. The watch began at 10:00 p.m., and it was the mayor and aldermen, and not the city marshal, who decided what weapons would be carried by the watchmen. Each watchman was paid one dollar per night worked.

There were thirty ships and sixty-four schooners tied up in Portsmouth in 1860. Frank Jones purchased English brewer John Swindles's beer-making business on Islington Street and formed the Frank Jones Ale Company. Within twenty years, Frank Jones would become the number one producer of beer in the world.

Like it is today, Portsmouth was visited by many people who significantly swelled the population and had an impact on police service. Navy sailors on shore leave from the navy yard, traders and fishermen representing an abundant maritime fleet and visiting businessmen and tourists would often be found in the local merchant shops, restaurants and bars. Portsmouth was a rough and seedy young city with many people in town to drink alcohol, visit prostitutes, gamble or otherwise spend their money on life's vices. The police were struggling with erratic leadership, no job security, few written rules and haphazard police procedures. Yet through all this, they managed to provide the level of police protection the community needed.

A schooner painting on the wall as you enter Portsmouth City Hall. *Photo by the author.*

The Civil War period (1861–65) brought greater prosperity to Portsmouth as shipbuilding thrived and the area bustled with soldiers[165] and sailors looking to spend their leave money. There were 120 drinking saloons in 1864, along with thirty houses of ill fame to attend to men's desires. The city council increased the pay of police officers from $50 per year to $600 per year, with the marshal's pay increased from $600 to $800 per year. The railroad thrived, and a large railroad station was built off Deer Street to accommodate the travelers and freight. The city purchased its first fire steam pumper in 1864, shortly after another great fire, this one starting at a paint shop on Penhallow Street and ending on Linden Street, or present-day Daniel Street, near the Federal Building.

The great abolitionist Frederick Douglass had already made two trips to deliver speeches in Portsmouth by 1862, and the police were on hand in July 1863 when the national Enrollment Act was passed by Congress.[166] Also known as the Draft Act and intended to conscript fresh men for the Union army, it sparked riots in many cities,[167] including Portsmouth. This act allowed a policy of substitution whereby any person so drafted could be excused by furnishing an equal replacement or by paying the government $300. This provision was designed to diminish resentment from antiwar supporters who would not fight. Instead, it caused bitter anger from those who were supporting the war but did not want to leave their farms and businesses but also could not afford the $300 payment or had no equal replacement. The slogan "rich man's war, poor man's fight" sounded in the streets and served to rally a small, unorganized mob of two hundred people who marched to Fort Constitution but were turned back by the organized guards.

Re-forming at Water Street, and quite drunk, the lawless crowd continued its rally and was met by the police, who had been reinforced with the auxiliary police. They were detailed with orders to prevent the crowd from gathering near the home of the provost marshal. Between eight and nine o'clock in the evening, the police made several arrests, with one being a known agitator named Sampson L. Russell, who also had his gun seized by a police officer. Russell called out to his friends in the crowd for help as he was being brought to the jail, and the mob responded and rallied around the prisoner. He was rescued from the arrest, but his gun was not found, and the horde thought it was still in the hands of the police. Later that night, Russell and Richard Walden rallied the mob to city hall and the police department, demanding the return of the gun. When the demand was refused, Walden attacked auxiliary police officer George Frenton with a long, square iron bolt. Frenton warded off the blow that was aimed at his head but suffered a painful wound to his arm and wrist. Walden was then heard to shout, "Fire!" followed by the sounds of gunshots.

Mayor Dearborn had already been summoned by Marshal Bragdon to respond to the uprising. The mayor arrived just as the first shots rang out, and he immediately summoned a detail of marines from the navy yard, as well as the garrison at Fort Constitution, to respond immediately to help break up the mob. As the marines approached, they could be heard marching in cadence with the "faint gleam of their bayonets…seen." The hundred or so protestors took off running "like sheep, taking the wounded with them." Russell (the man who had escaped earlier) was found and rearrested. He suffered from a severe head wound, apparently "inflicted…by a watchman's hook." Four others involved in organizing and inciting the mob were also arrested, but in the end, none was tried. When it was over, Officer Frank B. Johnson discovered his close call with death when he found a bullet hole in the hat he was wearing. The bullet had passed within an inch of his head, entering the front of the hat and exiting out the top. The *Portsmouth Gazette* newspaper opined, "All honor to the police for their energetic action, and to the military for their active cooperation."

Helmet worn by the Portsmouth Police, on display at the Portsmouth Police Department. *Photo by the author.*

Another demonstration that had the police involved occurred the day after the end of the Civil War. It was raining on April 10, 1865, when a large crowd of drunk citizens, sailors, merchant seamen and shipyard workers formed to destroy the office of the antiwar and proslavery *States and Union* newspaper on Daniel Street. Joshua Foster was the owner and editor, and he was attending to his duties when the crowd of two thousand showed up threatening to lynch him.[168] Foster escaped out the back door, and the outnumbered police officers stood by out front and watched as this mass of people threw office files, furniture and even the printing press out the second-

floor windows. The provost marshal arrived from the shipyard and convinced the people to leave, with many of them walking toward Market Square or back to the saloons to continue celebrating the end of the war. Foster would later sue the city and the navy yard for their negligence in controlling the mob. He would lose his suit against the city but was awarded $2,000 from the navy yard, which he used to rebuild his newspaper business. Within seven years, he founded the present-day *Foster's Daily Democrat* newspaper.

Later that year, the police would be outfitted in blue uniforms.[169] The city clarified the power of the city marshal by specifically writing that total command and authority of all the assistant marshals, police officers, night watchmen, constables and auxiliary police officers would be under his sole command. Up to this point, police officers had been subject to the orders of both their commanding officers and the mayor. Under this ordinance, the city marshal would still answer to and serve at the will of the mayor,[170] but the officers would have some political protection from the mayor and a more streamlined chain of command by answering only to the city marshal. The pay for the city marshal was also increased to $800.00 per year, with the assistant marshals, constables and police officers receiving $600.00 per year. The auxiliary police officers would still be paid $1.50 per day worked.

Wool police overcoat worn by the Portsmouth Police on daily patrol until the early 1970s, on display at the Portsmouth Police Department. *Photo by the author.*

It would be police misconduct in November 1865 that was blamed for a destructive fire. It was determined that the night watch police officers retired early, at 4:00 a.m., and shortly thereafter, a fire started that burned down the Congress Street block. Had the officers been on duty, they might have been able to take actions that would have limited the amount of damage. The Portsmouth Police, to this day, have a duty to serve as an attentive fire watch and to sound the hue and cry of "Fire!" when spotted. In 1865, this would have been done by shouting or using a rattle[171] or whistle to gain attention and to call the community to action. The officers had few tools available at their immediate disposal to deal with a fire. Today, raising a warning is done via digital police radio to a police dispatcher who notifies the fire department. The police cruisers are outfitted with powerful portable fire extinguishers, and the officers are trained in basic firefighting to better improve the chances of putting out a fire or limiting its destruction until the arrival of the fire department.

The new uniforms required to be worn in 1865 were the subject of outgoing city marshal J. Horace Kent's[172] report to incoming marshal Frank B. Johnson. He noted, "It has been the pleasure of the entire police force to uniform themselves in a neat suit of blue with appropriate brass buttons, which adds very much to their appearance and efficiency." Across the world, there was increased interest in crime and law enforcement, which helped initiate many changes to existing police organizations, including the Portsmouth Police Department. There were poems being written—such as George W. Matsell's "A Hundred Stretches Hence"—that used the word "cop" as slang for police.[173] The *National Police Gazette* featured many articles about brutal murders, kidnappings and odd robberies. Edgar Allan Poe wrote his detective whodunits during this time, to include "The Murders in the Rue Morgue" (1841) and the "Purloined Letter" (1844–45). The fictional Sherlock Holmes made his first appearance in 1887, bringing the interest of crime, punishment and the police investigator to the everyday person. People all over were becoming more educated and interested in the work of the police, and expectations of the level of police services within communities increased.

In New York, six police matrons were hired to watch over the female inmates on Blackwell Island, while Matthew Brady was photographing prisoners and examining them to see if there were physical commonalities among criminals. The San Francisco Police were grouping photographs into collections to help identify criminals to the public. Police in Switzerland were documenting crime scenes with photographs, while London's Metropolitan Police published its rules and regulations for police officers, including Warrant Number 1, which dismissed a police officer for being drunk on duty.

Officer William Smart. *Image the property of the Portsmouth Athenaeum, used with permission.*

The Chicago Police formed a detective division in 1860, along with installing police call boxes and signals in 1861.[174] The lawless town of Deadwood, South Dakota, was averaging one murder a day in 1876, and Thailand disbanded its secret police and introduced a more modern and open police force. In India in 1866, Sir George William Robert Campbell required that all police officers take a proficiency exam, follow written directives and be promoted not because of politics or favoritism but by an impartial selection process based on merit. The British introduced traffic control devices in 1868, and the first United States National Police Convention was held in St. Louis, Missouri, in 1871.

Professionalism and standardization were possible and being demanded by communities. When Scotland Yard discovered some members accepting bribes from a gang of gambling criminals, it immediately dismissed these detectives and charged them criminally.[175] In 1889, Ghent, Belgium, formed the first police canine training academy, which prepared thirty-seven dogs to help police its 170,000 inhabitants. The dogs would walk on patrol with the constables from 10:00 p.m. to daybreak. By 1890, there was talk of forming a Portsmouth Police Commission to improve police services and equipment in the city.[176] An 1890 Portsmouth report offered insight into problems within the police department created by a high turnover rate that was caused by newly elected officials. These officials would remove from service

Unknown Portsmouth Police officer. *Image the property of the Portsmouth Police Department, used with permission.*

City Marshal Charles W. Norton (1884–1886). *Image the property of the Portsmouth Police Department, used with permission.*

those police officers who did not support them in the local election and commission those who had supported them. It summarized, "Long service is essential so that the ways of the classes who come in contact with this department, should be studied and kept track of. We found the whole system in vogue, in a completely demoralized condition, and the custom which followed out at the commencement of the year in a great measure of removals was not what should be in the size City such as ours. The Officers were with two or three exceptions all new men and had a great deal to learn."

A board of police commissioners was formed by the aldermen (city council). Three people were selected—two from one political party and the third from the other. Favoritism continued right through this new paper layer of appointed men, and within five years, the people demanded real change. The call rang out to empower the governor to select the police commissioners so the officers were not subject to the "mutations of [local] politics" and to help improve the Portsmouth Police Department.

THE MURDER OF PRISONER CANTY BY OFFICER SMITH

The start of the centennial election day on March 14, 1876, was similar to previous election days, but it ended in a very unusual and tragic manner. That Tuesday began with Marshal Israel Marden activating the Auxiliary Police force to help ensure that Portsmouth would remain peaceful and that the election would take place without any voter fraud, political intimidation or outright polling place violence.[177] Officer Andrew J. Smith was assigned to keep the peace at the Christian Shore polling places for Wards 1 and 7 along with Officer Glazebrook.[178] At about 3:30 p.m., the polling places were closed, and Officers Smith and Glazebrook decided to enter Ayers's Store,[179] where they found a large crowd inside. Smith particularly noticed a man who was angry and having a "fit" and was trying to start a fight with another man in the store.

Officer Edmund Clark Jr. was a two-year full-time veteran of the police force. He was nearby, walking his beat, when he heard the commotion from Ayers's Store and went to investigate. Inside, he noticed Officer Smith trying to calm a man he knew to be William Canty, a workman at Jones's Brewery and considered to be "the most powerful [physically toughest] man in the city," according to the *Portsmouth Daily Chronicle* of March 16, 1876. Officer Clark took over from Officer Smith, ordering a very drunk Canty to keep quiet and to stop his provocation toward others in the room. Canty did not calm down and continued his fighting attitude. After several more attempts by Officer Clark to quell the "free fight," Clark arrested Canty. Several of Canty's friends were inside the store as well and tried to rescue Canty, but the officers succeeded

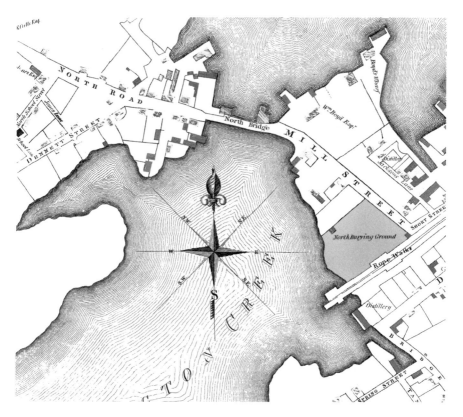

Map of Dennett Street, where Ayers's Store was located, and the North Bridge area, where Canty shoved Officers Smith and Glazebrook. *Used with permission of William T. and Constance Warren.*

in placing their suspect in the "twisters."[180] The officers warded off Canty's friends and brought Canty outside the store, but not before Canty threw Officer Clark out the open door and onto the sidewalk. Officer Clark picked himself up and then directed Officers Smith and Glazebrook to bring Canty to the police station,[181] about three-quarters of a mile away, while Clark continued to deal with Canty's very upset friends.

Officers Smith and Glazebrook started heading to the station with their prisoner, but a short distance away,[182] Canty shoved both officers aside, pushing them into a tree with considerable force. Canty was able to free himself from the twisters with a "strong jerk" and struck a blow to Officer Glazebrook's head, which Glazebrook was able to partially block. As Canty approached Smith to strike the officer, Smith drew his billy club from his belt and hit Canty once in the head with a glancing blow. This blow did not stop Canty's fighting behavior, and Smith struck him again in the right side of the

Right: Portsmouth Police "twisters" with a leather belt holder. *On display at the Portsmouth Police Department. Photo by the author.*

Below: Short lead-weighted billy club used by the Portsmouth Police. *On display at the Portsmouth Police Department. Photo by the author.*

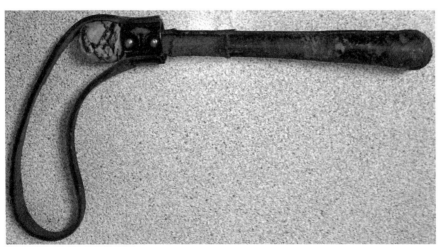

head. When this second blow did not stop Canty, Smith hit him a third time, and this time Canty stopped fighting and fell to the ground.[183] Canty rubbed his head. He was then brought to his feet by the officers and quietly walked with them to the station house, occasionally talking with them and wiping the blood away from his head.

Jail cell in the Portsmouth Police Station on Penhallow Street. It was formally the Rockingham County Jail. *Image the property of the Portsmouth Police Department, used with permission.*

When Canty arrived at the police station, he was greeted by Officer Hobbs, who helped Canty clean the dried blood from his head with cold water. Hobbs then escorted Canty to the jail cell, where Canty tried to punch Hobbs but missed. Canty was locked in the cell, and Hobbs checked on him fifteen minutes later, noticing that Canty was sleeping quietly on the top bunk. Canty's friends arrived at the police station to plead with City Marshal Marden to release him, but the marshal saw that Canty was resting quietly and felt he needed to spend more time in the cell to sober up before going home. Shortly after supper, Canty's friends returned, asking again for Canty's release because he needed to go to work at nine thirty that night.

The marshal agreed to release Canty, and Officers Hobbs and Halloran went to the cell. They noticed that Canty was still asleep but breathing heavily. They tried to wake him, but something was wrong; Canty would not get up. Officer Watkins was ordered to fetch Dr. Potter immediately. Dr.

Potter was able to revive Canty with some cold water, and Canty was released to his friends. They walked the big man home to his father's (Godfrey Canty) house.[184] Canty slept the rest of the evening at his father's house, and when the family checked his bed shortly before five o'clock the next morning, William Canty was dead.

All suspicious deaths at that time were investigated by a coroner's inquest, and the death of William Canty was no different. The very same day that William Canty died, Coroner John E. Ryder empaneled Justice of the Peace George E. Hodgdon, Josiah G. Hadley and James F. Hartshorn, all "reputable people," to hear evidence and render an opinion of the cause of death of William Canty. For the next two days, twenty witnesses would be sworn in and heard on this matter. There was no dispute over the relevant facts of the case. All agreed that William Canty was a man of great strength; he had been drunk and in a fighting mood and was deserving of the arrest. All agreed that Canty fought with "cool and collected" arresting officers and had tried to escape arrest several times. Those who saw the attempted escape while Canty was being walked to the station agreed that Canty continued to be violent. Officer Smith had used his billy club to subdue Canty in self-defense and in defense of his partner, Officer Glazebrook. It was also undisputed that Canty died from a fractured skull and broken blood vessels caused by the billy club blows to the head. The only unclear fact was exactly how many times Officer Smith struck Canty, but it was determined to be somewhere between three and six times.

The inquest centered on the standard legal use of force that would allow the police to strike a person in self-defense or while making an arrest. In 1876, this standard required police officers to first call out for help and summon bystanders to render immediate aid when needed. Those who did not come to the aid of a police officer could be charged and arrested because it was a citizen's legal duty to assist the police when summoned.

When Canty broke away from Officers Smith and Glazebrook and tried to make good his escape by further attacking them, the officers did not call out for help, nor did they summon the various bystanders to assist them in regaining control of Canty. Several of these private citizens would testify that they surely would have rendered aid and were in a position to deliver effective assistance to these officers. But instead of calling for help, Officer Smith took it upon himself to draw his club and hit Canty on the head.

Undated Portsmouth Police officers. *Image the property of the Portsmouth Athenaeum, used with permission.*

At four o'clock on the second day of the inquest, the jurors handed down the following verdict:

> ...*The said Andrew J. Smith did then and there with a certain weapon called a "Policeman's Billy"* [hit] *the said William Canty then and there feloniously and willfully in and upon the head of him...one mortal wound*

Complaint against Officer Smith. *Document from the property of the New Hampshire Division of Archives and Records Management, image scanned by the author.*

of which said mortal wound the said William Canty from said Fourteenth day of March until the Fifteenth day of the same March did languish and languishing did live on which said fifteenth day of March…did die and so the complainant aforesaid says the said Andrew J. Smith…there kill and slay.

Signed John E. Ryder

Officer Smith was immediately arrested for manslaughter by City Marshal Marden. Smith was brought the next day before Justice Calvin Page of the Portsmouth Police Court, where Smith pleaded not guilty and bail was set at $1,500. Officer Smith returned to jail for three more days, until March 20, when surety bail was posted on his behalf "to the satisfaction of the Judge of the Police Court of Portsmouth." Less than one month later, on April 15, 1876, the grand jury indicted Smith for manslaughter, and the superior court trial was scheduled to begin two weeks later, on April 27.

The community reacted strongly in defense of Officer Smith. The *Portsmouth Chronicle* newspaper editorialized before the trial:

> *Not a particle of evidence, so far as we know, was introduced to show that Smith was actuated by anger, or that he intended to kill Canty, or to do anything more than defend his mate—which in this case, we take it, was precisely the same as defending himself. A blow from a man of Canty's great strength would have been serious if not a fatal affair to the recipient; and that the safety of the public and the peace of the city imperatively demanded his being restrained at the time we think no one will dispute. The only question that arises in our mind is whether the officer acted rightly in depending upon himself and his club to quell the belligerence of the prisoner, or should have called upon private citizens for help; and while we cannot but regret that one man lost his life and another is placed in a most painful situation in consequence of the officer relying upon his own resources, we think he would not have been justified in calling upon outside aid. The police are paid to protect citizens from law-breakers; citizens are not paid for protecting the police; and an officer who calls for help from citizens before he has tried all the means in his power to help himself, does not do his duty and has no business on the force. The officer's first duty is to protect the law-observing private citizen from outrage and all hazards, though he risk or even lose his life in so doing; his second duty is to protect himself; but it is no part of his duty to call upon private citizens to aid him in case of trouble until he becomes assured he can not preserve the peace unaided.*

An identified citizen wrote to the editors of the *Portsmouth Daily Chronicle* on April 18, 1876, asking:

> *Was Smith justified in using any force to take his prisoner to the station house? If he was not, then the appointment of a police force is a ridiculous farce; if he was justified in using any force at all, he was certainly justified in using all the force necessary. If an officer may properly use forcible means to restrain a law-breaker, it must of course be at the law-breaker's risk, not at the officer's.*

Officer Smith would be represented by Attorney Marston of Exeter and Attorney Page of Portsmouth, the latter being the same man who had served as judge at his arraignment. Attorney Frank Hatch prosecuted the case for

Unknown Portsmouth police officer. *Image the property of the Portsmouth Athenaeum, used with permission.*

the state, and the trial would last ten days. The jury was given the case to deliberate on Tuesday, May 2, 1876. Forty minutes later, the jurors returned with a verdict: acquittal.[185] The spectators in the gallery burst into applause; however, Officer Smith's name would never again appear on the police work roster. His days as a police officer were over.

DRUNKEN COPS AND THE POLICE COMMISSION

After a half century of official existence, the police department in Portsmouth was thick with corruption, drunken cops on duty, men who would sleep instead of making their proscribed midnight rounds through Market Square and a general neglect of duty that allowed a dozen brothels to freely exist. A police commission log entry in 1895 acknowledged and addressed police misconduct in this manner: "At a meeting of the police commission it was voted to notify the marshal to publically [*sic*] reprimand Captain Marden of the night police in the presence of the whole force for neglect of duty."[186] Officer W.H. Anderson was given a one-month suspension on June 20, 1901, for being drunk on duty, followed by the suspension of Officers Murphy, Shannon and Burns[187] a few months later. The police commission, on July 13, 1901, ordered Marshal Entwistle:

> *You are directed by unanimous vote of the Board of Police Commissioners to inform every officer employed on the Portsmouth, N.H. Police Force that the use of any and all intoxicating drinks is strictly prohibited while on duty and any Officer who is known to be intoxicated while on duty will be immediately discharged and when discharged for said offense from said Force said discharge will be final—John E. Demmick, Clerk.*

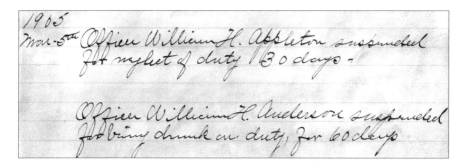

1905

Mar. 5th Officer William H. Appleton suspended for neglect of duty 30 days –

Officer William H. Anderson suspended for being drunk on duty, for 60 days

City Marshal Entwistle's 1905 log outlining the suspension of Officer Anderson for being drunk on duty. *Property of the Portsmouth Police, scanned by the author.*

Moreover, whenever there was an election that decided a new mayor, the police force would change because the new mayor replaced the police commissioners and police officers who did not support him in the election. The 1890 City Report expressed:

> *When good, sober, intelligent officers are in, it would seem wise policy they should be retained: for the efficiency of the service depends upon experience, and attention to detail…there should be no discharges from the Force for political reasons.*

But Portsmouth was not alone when it came to political favoritism. In 1893, New Hampshire communities, such as Manchester and Concord, had their mayors stripped of the authority to select police officers when the New Hampshire legislature voted to have the governor, along with the governor's council, appoint local police commissioners who would assume the powers of the mayor in matters of the police department. This act removed the ability of the mayor to hire and fire the police officers and brought about greater stability in these police forces. The Portsmouth Police's political favoritism was addressed as well in 1895, when the state legislature passed an act that had the governor and his council appoint three local men to serve as police commissioners and set the number of police officers and their rate of pay. The state law gave total control of the police department to the commissioners, to include the hiring, firing, promoting and seemingly more controversial setting of the annual budget to be paid by the Portsmouth taxpayers.

Portsmouth had 10,637 inhabitants and was a central city in New England politically, culturally and economically. Though it was fast losing its prestige as an industrial leader to textile and shoe communities—like Manchester, Nashua and Concord—along the Merrimack River, it still had one of the

Portsmouth Police officer wearing the "radiator-style" badge. *Image the property of the Portsmouth Athenaeum, used with permission.*

largest beer manufacturers in the world in the Frank Jones Ale Company. Portsmouth also boasted its own shoe factory along Islington Street, a button factory and manufacturers of instruments such as organs and pianos. The Portsmouth Naval Shipyard, established in 1800 as the first naval shipyard in the country, was busy making warships, as well as housing the surviving heroes of the Greely Arctic Expedition. These explorers had been sent to collect scientific data and to map the most northern regions of the earth, but they were shipwrecked on the ice for three years. They were finally rescued and brought to the shipyard to recover.[188]

In 1898, about 1,300 prisoners of the Spanish-American War were also housed at the shipyard on the grounds of Camp Long, which, ten years later, would be the site of the world's largest poured concrete building, called the "The Castle" or the Portsmouth Naval Shipyard Prison.[189] "Old Ironsides," or the USS *Constitution*, was docked at the shipyard and served as a floating dormitory for sea cadets. Elsewhere around town, a person could get a wool suit on sale from the Henry Peyser and Son store for $7.75, and a cigar cost $0.10. "Dirt's worst enemy" and "A woman's best friend" both described Fairbanks Washing Powder, as advertised in the *Portsmouth Herald* in 1898, and coal could be purchased from O.F. Philbrick & Company at 4 Water Street. There was a general hue and cry for the police department to do something about the numbers of unlicensed dogs loose in the Bowery and White Chapel Districts. In response, the police hired Harry E. Givens as dog catcher and Joseph Hett as dog keeper/executioner, to be paid $1.00 for each dog caught and killed.

Police departments in general were maturing and started to offer the officers stability in their jobs and improved working conditions in exchange

The Rockingham County Jail in Portsmouth after construction in 1891. It would be used as the jail until 1953, when it was turned over to the city for use as its police station. This building would house the police officers until 1991. *Image the property of the Portsmouth Police Department and Strawbery Banke, used with permission.*

The 1953 Portsmouth Police Station. *Image the property of the Portsmouth Police Department, used with permission.*

The coal wharf area looking toward State and Water Streets. *Image the property of the Portsmouth Athenaeum, used with permission.*

for an increase in professionalism, work product and a higher standard of ethics. The first steps toward reform in Portsmouth came in 1895, with the New Hampshire legislature's establishment of Portsmouth Police commissioners,

Portsmouth Police officer George Carlton. *Image the property of the Portsmouth Athenaeum, used with permission.*

who were expected to lessen the apparent negative local political influence.[190] The legislature also set the number of Portsmouth Police officers at no more than twenty, along with establishing their pay at $2.50 per day worked.[191] These officers were commanded by a captain of the night watch, an assistant city marshal and the city marshal. Their pay would be the same as the officers': $2.50 per day worked, except for the marshal, who would get $1,000 per year.[192] Taking away the city council control, or home rule, of the police department infuriated many of the local citizens, including Mayor William O. Junkins, who stated in his inaugural address:

> *Under the best form of republican government, which is the boast of the United States of America, home rule and local self government have ever been the fundamental principles dearest to the people, and in the great struggle for home rule which Ireland has been carrying on against England for so many years, the Irish have had the sympathy and pecuniary aid of nearly every Citizen of the United States, regardless of politics, sect or religion. It is natural therefore that every good Citizen who believes in the form of government under which we live, should view with alarm this attempt to deprive our City of the right of self government, and set up in our midst against the will of the Citizens a body of uniformed officials to enforce and execute the laws, over whom the Citizens and their representatives—the City Councils—have no control, and in whose election they have no voice. The Governor of this State, living in a distant city, and the legislature, composed of men residing elsewhere, a few of them taxpayer here or interested in our City, determine who shall constitute our Police Force,*

Portrait of Mayor Junkins that hangs in the Portsmouth City Council chambers. *Photo by the author.*

87

how many officers we shall have, and what amount we shall be taxed in order to pay them, and we are as powerless as our fathers were before the Revolution, when they were governed without their consent by the officials sent over from Great Britain by the King which caused them to assert that great truth, set forth in the Declaration of Independence, that "Governments can only derive their just powers from the consent of the governed."

There was fear among the local politicians that they would lose their local power and be ruled by the governor at the state level. The appointment of a police commission was the start of that slippery slope. As Mayor Junkins continued in his city address of 1895:

If the Legislature and the Governor can set up a Police Commission, no reason occurs to me why they cannot appoint a Commission to control every other Municipal Department, and the annual election of a Mayor and City Councils will be useless proceeding and a farce, and the so called right of suffrage, an unmeaning and ineffective form…I am sure that a large majority of our Citizens are opposed to a Police Commission. It is un-democratic and un-republican. It is un-American and unjust. It is destructive of home rule and local self government. It is taxation without representation and government without the consent of the governed. It is abhorrent to every independent, liberty loving Citizen, and when the system has been extended to our highways and streets our Fire Department, and our other municipal affairs, as it is liable to be unless it is opposed and defeated here and now, we shall be at the mercy of partisan Legislatures, unscrupulous State officials, and selfish combinations of persons not inhabitants of the City, and the government of our City will be no less a tyranny than that of any monarchy or despotism in the world.

Despite the mayor's objection and his calling the governor-appointed police commission "un-democratic and un-republican…un-American and unjust," on April 2, 1895, three men were appointed by Governor Charles A. Busiel of Laconia and confirmed by his council as Portsmouth Police commissioners. The first commissioners were William H. Sise (chairman), John E. Demmick (clerk) and Ira C. Seymour, with the pay fixed at $300 for the chairman and $100 each for the others. The *Portsmouth Journal* wrote:

The gentlemen composing it are all well known and respected citizens, and it is hoped and believed that they will so manage affairs as to justify their

The

State of New Hampshire,

To John E. Dimick Esquire Greeting

Know you, That we, reposing especial trust and confidence in your Fidelity and ability, have constituted and appointed you Police Commissioner for the city of Portsmouth Hereby giving and granting unto you, the said

John E Dimick

all the power and authority given and granted by the Constitution and Laws of our State to a Commission as as aforesaid To have and to hold the said office with all the powers, privileges and immunities to the same belonging, for the term of Six years from and after April 2nd 1895, provided you are of good behavior during said term.

In Testimony whereof we have caused our seal to be hereunto affixed.

Witness Charles A Busiel Governor of our State at Concord this nineteenth day of February in the year of our Lord one thousand eight hundred and ninety five and of the Independence of the United States of America the one hundred and nineteenth.

By his excellency the Governor, with advice of the Council

Charles A Busiel
Governor

Ezra S Stearns
Secretary of State

Warrant establishing the Portsmouth Police Commission in 1895. *Property of the Portsmouth Police Department on loan to the Portsmouth Athenaeum, scanned by the author, used with permission.*

selection and fulfill the promises made by their sponsors, that they will give our citizens a clean, able and business-like administration. Upon them rests great responsibility. That they will so order things here as to merit general praise, we confidently prophesy.

Commissioner John E. Demmick, one of the first Portsmouth police commissioners, 1895. *Image the property of the Portsmouth Police Department, used with permission.*

Mayor Junkins did not agree with this, and his reaction to this well-intentioned legislative act would bring about several of the most volatile months for the police department. Angered over the move, the mayor did not allow the police commissioners or their police officers to staff the police station, which was housed in city hall. In fact, Mayor Junkins did not disband the existing police department and ordered it to stay on duty. The *Portsmouth Journal* called this move "Cry Baby Tactics" and called the mayor's police force "illegal, disgraceful, incendiary and dangerous, and will not be tolerated by [the] law abiding majority of our citizens." Forced to find a headquarters, the police commissioners worked out of the Rockingham County Courthouse,[193] located on State Street, and ordered the City of Portsmouth to pay the rent "for the use of the rooms… and a portion of the Jail for the Officers appointed by us." For the next six weeks, Portsmouth would be policed by two separate police departments, one housed at city hall under Mayor Junkins and the other out of the courthouse under the police commissioners.

It took the local Portsmouth election of 1895 to decide the matter. Republican Frank J. Philbrick voiced his strong support of the police commission and ended up defeating Mayor Junkins in the May election. By May 18, 1895, the *Portsmouth Journal* reported "a fresh start" as the city "formally withdraws all opposition and agrees to give up the police station." In something out of a modern-day movie scene, Commissioner Sise, City Marshal Butterfield and his police officers marched up the police station steps at city hall at high noon to receive the office keys from outgoing city marshal Rowe. And so ended the dual police forces within the city.

This would not be the end to a controversial year, though. Within a few months, the police commissioners and Marshal Butterfield were in

The first police commission meeting notes. *Property of the Portsmouth Police Department, scanned by the author.*

disagreement about how to clean up the disorderly areas of the Bowery and Water Street. Manchester, New Hampshire, had recently taken the approach of strict enforcement of liquor laws as a means of curbing rowdy and disorderly behavior, and the Portsmouth Police commissioners argued that City Marshal Butterfield should take this same approach. The commissioners wanted him to perform more raids on the saloons, especially on Sundays, when the sale of all liquor was illegal. The commissioners went public with their plan "to reduce the number of places where liquor is sold by steady continued raids, closing the least respectable saloons as fast as possible; no new places will be allowed to open, and a place once closed must remain so and no other person, no matter how respectable, will be allowed to open it." Marshal Butterfield did not agree with these priorities and instead asked the newly appointed police commission for "a

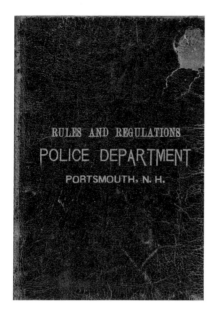 

Left: 1890 *Rules and Regulations* book. *On display at the Portsmouth Police Department, scanned by the author.*

Right: Portsmouth Police badge, circa 1880. *On display at the Portsmouth Police Department, scanned by the author.*

remedy of existing evil" after sixteen women were arrested in three months and forced to be jailed in "quarters that are a disgrace to a civilized community."

Other issues the marshal pointed out that plagued the department and required the more immediate attention of the police commission were:

- Only one copy of the department rules and regulations could be found for the entire department to use. He wanted one printed for each officer to carry on duty.
- The department lacked the necessary number of badges and revolvers.
- The badge of the city marshal was privately owned and cost $3.50. He recommended that one be purchased by the police department to be worn by the current city marshal but would continue to be owned by the city.
- Parade equipment needed to be borrowed from sister cities. None was owned by the city.
- Internal rules and regulations were not enforced.
- Officers were not always working in regulation uniform.

Portsmouth Police on parade. *Image the property of the Portsmouth Police Department, used with permission.*

- Officers were not required to make a report on things that happened on their watch.
- A police electrical signal had to be implemented for the Creek patrol officer who was over one mile away from the police station and needed to be able to communicate with those in the station. The current means of using the Brewery and Shoe Factory telephones took too much time and required the officer to come off his beat. An additional electrical signal needed to be placed on Market Street and one on Water Street.
- The distribution of "hand bills and dodgers" about the street were a nuisance.
- The police were tasked with enforcing snow removal in front of shops that had sidewalks. The police expressed "trouble" in enforcement of this law, which required the police to serve notice to any shopkeeper who did not clean the sidewalk in front of his shop.

The marshal soon fell into disfavor with the commissioners, who were seeking out a new city marshal by October 1895. Enter Thomas Entwistle, a stout man with a big, bushy blond mustache. He was born in Hyde, England, on January 12, 1840, and was brought to this country at an early age. At age nine, to help support the family, he began to work in the

Lamont Hilton. *Image the property of the Portsmouth Athenaeum, used with permission.*

Portsmouth steam textile mills as a bobbin boy.[194] He was twenty-one years old when he enlisted in the Third New Hampshire Volunteers to fight in the Civil War. He was wounded twice and captured at Drury's Bluff by the Confederates, who confined him in the notorious Andersonville Prison.[195] He escaped and found his way back to Portsmouth, where he became a police officer in 1867 and was promoted to city marshal in 1877. He was one of the investigators of the 1873 Smuttynose Island murders[196] but later

Above: Cellblock key used by the Portsmouth Police. *On display at the Portsmouth Police Department. Photo by the author.*

Right: City Marshal Entwistle. *Image the property of the Portsmouth Police Department, used with permission.*

gave up his city marshal position in 1884 to work as a blacksmith at the Portsmouth Naval Shipyard. Police commissioners Demmick and Seymour courted him to rejoin the force as city marshal and to carry out their reform plan. Commissioner Sise also grew tired of Marshal Butterfield but instead wanted current assistant city marshal Hilton to take over as marshal. The issue was forced on the commissioners on October 26, 1895, when Marshal Butterfield resigned, effective October 30, 1895.

In a year that saw the Warwick Club celebrate its third anniversary,[197] an investigation into the padded cell death of prisoner Timothy F. Cronin[198] and two police departments policing the same city, Police Commissioners Demmick and Seymour voted to name Thomas Entwistle as city marshal, effective November 25, 1895. The *Portsmouth Journal* reported on November 30, "He is tough on selling beer on Sundays." While he might have been tough on illegal alcohol sales and intoxication, he would turn many blind eyes to the dozen brothels in and along Water Street.[199] The arrest log of 1897 does not document any arrest entries for "keeping a disorderly house" or "prostitution"—only one arrest in 1898 for "disorderly house"—and Entwistle largely ignored the December 13, 1894 Alderman Phinney resolution to "notify all proprietors of 'House of Ill Fame' to close by January 1, 1895, the Law to be enforced after that date."

HOOKERS OF THE BOWERY

I t was the 1890s, and the powerful Frank Jones was owner and president of many of the businesses in Portsmouth. As one of the world leaders in beer manufacturing[200] with his Frank Jones Ale, he employed more than five hundred people at his brewery along Islington Street. Jones used these beer sales profits to incorporate the Portsmouth Shoe Company, to rebuild the burnt Woodbury Langdon House into the current-day Rockingham Hotel building and to create electric companies such as the Rockingham Power and Light Company that would provide electricity to much of New Hampshire and southern Maine. He was a railroad baron, director of several banks and a newspaper publisher. He loved politics, often mixing his business interests with running for a certain political office. He would serve as a two-term mayor and a U.S. congressman, and he thought nothing of proposing laws that would benefit his businesses. He built a majestic mansion on Maplewood Avenue, with much of it still standing today.

Frank Jones loved to entertain, and although married, he had a weakness for the ladies. There is strong evidence to suggest that he had an affair with Delana B. Curtis, his personal assistant. There is also the prevailing thought that he liked the brothels that had cropped up around the gritty docks of Water Street because they were good for entertaining his many male customers who would visit from afar to conduct business deals. He even had frescoes painted on the ceilings of several of the rooms at the Rockingham Hotel, which he owned, so that the ladies would have something to look at while "entertaining." Water Street's red-lighted,

WITH THE POLICE

— —

The Officers Experience the Toughest Night of the Winter So Far.

Last night was a corker for the police officers, who were forced to travel around through the sleet and rain with the nastiest walking they have experienced so far this winter. They were kept busy also dodging snowslides and broken limbs from trees. But two arrests were made during the evening, and these were both sailors who created a disturbance at Philbrick hall during the dance and were arrested by Officer Murphy.

Six lodgers were taken care of at headquarters last evening and helped Captain Marden shovel off around the city building this morning.

Newspaper clipping of the January 1, 1898 police log. *Unknown newspaper. Image the property of the Portsmouth Police Department, used with permission.*

rum-hole reputation was known from New York to Hong Kong, according to author Kimbery Crisp, who wrote her master's thesis about her aunt Madam Alta Roberts.

These bordellos, now numbering at least a dozen, operated right under the watch of City Marshal Entwistle and seemingly with little trouble from his boys in blue. In what was called locally the "parade of whores," Madam Mary Baker would march newly arrived prostitutes through Market Square to her Glouster House brothel. For twenty-two years, Baker would dress up in her best red beehive-shaped wig, fancy clothes draped with furs, velvet choker and large brooch to lead what must have looked like the circus coming into town. She would greet her new girls while in her horse-drawn carriage at the train station on Deer Street and proudly march them in review through the center of town as advertisement that a new batch of hookers had arrived. The flamboyant "big cheese of Portsmouth madams" would smile at the navy seamen from the shipyard, local fishermen and the businessmen who lined the streets of the parade route, so close to her that bystanders could see the diamonds she had embedded in her two front gold teeth. Her Glouster House was described as having "mirrors on the ceiling and the rooms had little cubby holes…that's where the girls were. The house had a great big beautiful ballroom with a great big chandelier. There were red velvet curtains and paintings of bosomy nude women on the walls."

The year 1897 was especially good for business when as many as 1,500 sailors a day would cross the Piscataqua River[201] in "liberty parties" to drink in the saloons[202] and visit the cathouses named "Big" Etta DeForrest House,

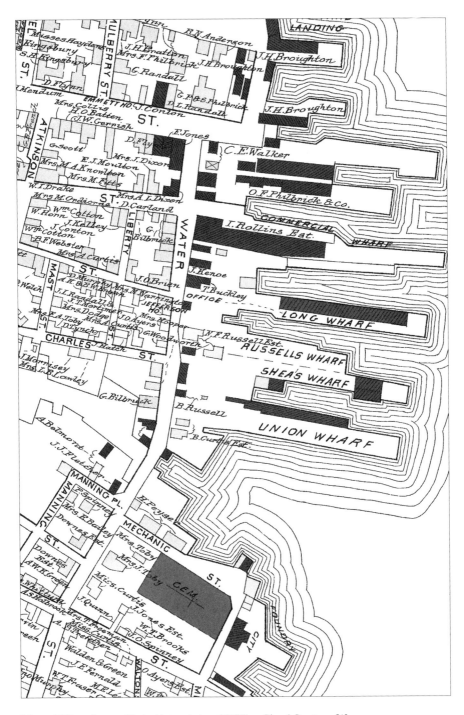

Map of Water Street. *Used with permission of William T. and Constance Warren.*

Looking down Water Street with the Glouster House on the corner. *Image the property of the Portsmouth Athenaeum, used with permission.*

State and Water (now called Marcy) Street today. The Glouster House has been torn down, and the waterfront wharfs have been removed. The area is now the home of Prescott Park. *Photo taken by Sergeant Chris Roth, used with permission.*

Ladies in front of the police station, 1902. *Image the property of the Portsmouth Police Department, used with permission.*

Commercial House, the Elm House, Glouster House and the Home and American House.[203] There was even a brothel on Four Tree Island,[204] listed officially as Four Tree Island Museum and Emporium, to which any man or workingwoman with a boat could come for a "visit." For those who lacked boats, a barge would shuttle them over to the big white house for a mere five cents. The ride back cost five dollars, but most were by then too boozed up to care. The island was also nicknamed the "Leper Colony" because it "catered to the lowest of the lowlifes," with its patrons gambling and betting on live cockfights. The building "was decorated with things that sailors had brought back from overseas, stuffed alligators, things like that. That's why he [owner Charles E. Gray] called it a museum. There was a stuffed cow at the bar, and you would pull the udders and booze would come out."[205] Gray showcased a pair of shoes worn by the outlaw Jesse James and enclosed the dance hall orchestra in a wire cage to protect it from the rowdy patrons. City Marshal Entwistle considered the island to be outside Portsmouth Police jurisdiction and refused to enforce city ordinances passed in 1853 pertaining to gambling and prostitution. While its remoteness proved effective in providing a habitat

"Houses of Suspended Integrity" along Water Street. *Image the property of the Portsmouth Athenaeum, used with permission.*

Sailors in a rowboat with the Four Tree Island Museum and Emporium in the middle and the Portsmouth Naval Shipyard in the background. *Image the property of the Portsmouth Athenaeum, used with permission.*

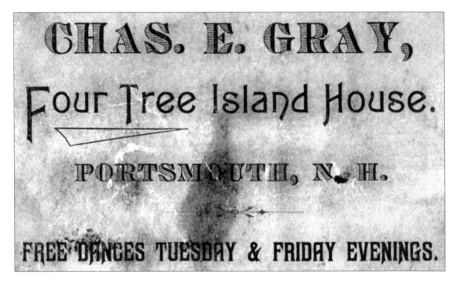

Top: Close-up of the Four Tree Island Museum and Emporium. *Image the property of the Portsmouth Athenaeum, used with permission.*

Middle: Advertisement handout card for the Four Tree Island Museum and Emporium. *Image the property of the Portsmouth Athenaeum, used with permission.*

Right: Advertisement handout card (backside) for the Four Tree Island Museum and Emporium. *Image the property of the Portsmouth Athenaeum, used with permission.*

LAST FALL.

A little horsehair sofa
In a corner stood,
Youth and maiden sparking,
So-fa—so good.

THIS SPRING.

A little baby in a crib,
Giving lots of bother,
Youthful mother making bib,
So-fa—no father.

for anarchy and debauchery, it also served in its demise when a fire in 1906 destroyed the museum and its contents because the firemen could not get out to the island in time to save them.

Madam Alta Roberts always wore black clothes when she was around her Elm House brothel. Perhaps she was also called the "little black mystery" because she lost her child giving birth, which prevented her from having any more children. Soon afterward, her husband died, and so, needing to earn a living, she went into the black-eyed profession of operating a house of ill repute. First operating 14 Water Street as a drinking saloon, she soon changed the building into "a dance hall where a three piece band would play." She would replace the pretty painted landscapes on the wall at night with those that depicted naked ladies. She would allow her girls, who were considered "such beautiful girls…they were so elegant and they were always dressed in the best clothes…they wore baby-doll pumps with round toes and spiked heels," to keep the two-dollar fee, which would serve as great enticement to farm girls looking to make money to support independent lifestyles in the city.

Cappy Stewart's brothel boasted sixteen ladies, whom he replaced every two to four weeks. His bordello had twenty-seven elegantly furnished rooms, complete with pornographic paintings that could retract into the wall at the push of a button. His rooms could be rented by the night or by the hour.[206] Even the local barber supplemented his income by having two prostitutes housed above the barbershop, catering to the carnal demands of sailors, fishermen, clergy, politicians, judges, business leaders, students from the nearby Phillips Exeter Academy and even police officer George Ducker, who would later become city marshal, and Judge William Marvin.

Prostitution was a thriving business in the shadiest part of town in the 1890s,[207] when Marshal Entwistle took over the police department. Marshal Entwistle would occasionally inspect, summon and fine proprietors for operating disorderly houses, but it was mostly with his sanction that the houses were allowed to operate.[208] There was talk that Marshal Entwistle would sometimes visit Madam Baker for more than just an "inspection." He was also seen hitching his horse team on Sundays and walking to each house to collect his graft.[209] It seemed that the community tolerated these homes, as well, because there was no public outrage when it was learned that Dr. George Pender, Dr. Herbert L. Taylor and Dr. Charles E. Johnson were openly being paid one dollar for each health inspection of the girls. After inspection, the girls were

Studio photo of Madam Alta Roberts and her family. *Back row, left to right*: Alta's nieces Ida McGinnis and Leona Hayward and Alta Roberts. *Front row, left*: Ida's husband, William McGinnis. The man in the bowler hat is unidentified. *Photo the property of Kimberly Crisp, used with permission.*

given certificates of health, which were required by madams like Mary Baker and Alta Roberts and were posted on the walls of each girl's room. These scurrilous activities were completely tolerated for more than fifteen

Auxiliary officer James A. Trueman, circa 1900. *Photo the property of the Portsmouth Police Department, scanned by the author, used with permission.*

years, until 1911, when several sailors were found dead after drinking in the red-light district.

On March 27, 1911, the battered and beaten body of marine Private Louis E. Rassmussen was found dead along the railroad tracks just over the railroad bridge in Kittery. It was determined that Rassmussen had been drinking at a Portsmouth saloon with his friend marine Corporal J.C. Ganson, and upon walking back drunk to the navy yard barracks, they engaged in a fight. Ganson was arrested and charged with manslaughter; he was tried on May 13, 1911. Ganson admitted to drinking two pints of rum with Rassmussen and getting into the fight with him along the walk back to the navy yard, but he was found not guilty of the manslaughter charge. The coroner ruled Rassmussen's death to be from alcohol-induced exposure.

Another body was fished from the river on August 22, 1911, and it was later identified as C.A. Danfourth by his father. It was determined that a month before, Danfourth had visited Portsmouth and returned in a drunken state to his ship, where he fell off the gangplank and into the river. A search was conducted that night, but he was not found. This drunken fatality served as yet another example the frustrated community used to show why Portsmouth needed to clean up the alcohol-induced troubles. Moreover, Officer Dennis Murphy was stabbed that same summer while he tried to arrest a construction worker involved in a domestic incident in the South End. It started when an angry thirty-three-year-old Italian immigrant named James Rossi punched a glass window during a domestic argument. Officer Murphy heard the breaking glass and, upon arrival in the area, learned that Rossi was the suspect but had left the house. Murphy quickly caught up with the bleeding Rossi and arrested him. While Murphy was escorting Rossi to the jail, Rossi broke free, brandished a knife and stabbed Murphy in the chest just above the heart and again in the hand as Murphy tried to fend off a second attack.[210] As Rossi fled, Murphy drew his revolver and shot at Rossi but missed, with the bullet striking a nearby fourteen-year-old boy in the leg. Officer Murphy was only slightly injured from the stab wounds; he was able to catch up with the fleeing Rossi and rearrested him.

Early handcuffs used by the Portsmouth Police. *On display at the Portsmouth Police Department. Photo by the author.*

Officer James McCaffery. He would serve forty-eight years as a Portsmouth Police officer. *Image the property of the Portsmouth Police Department, used with permission.*

The saloon areas reeked with the smell of alcohol and urine. Rats freely ran back and forth on the dirt roadways from the waterfront warehouses, and fistfights, with police firing warning shots from their revolvers, were frequent occurrences in 1911.[211] A man known as "Jack the Hugger" was dodging the police after routinely groping women in the downtown area, and the police commission was placing men like Samuel T. Drew on a "black list," which officially prevented licensed saloons from selling him any alcohol. In what seemed to be an effort to clean up the area and remove perceived individual police officer favoritism toward certain people and businesses, Marshal Entwistle issued General Order #210, which transferred every officer to a different beat. Entwistle quickly followed this with raids of the saloons along Market Street and ordered the closure of all of them in the area south of Deer Street to Market Square. This decision was met with the approval of the state liquor commission but would be overturned by the police commission just three days later.

Prostitution and alcohol were not the only vices that plagued Portsmouth at the time. Gambling, especially card playing and slot machines, was the subject of many police raids, and Entwistle conducted a "systematic crusade intended to root out the penny machines and other devices." On July 17, 1911, Entwistle led a raid on the Chinese restaurant on Deer Street, where he and Officers Shannon and West arrested nine "Chinamen" for gambling. The police commission addressed the police officers' gambling after several officers were caught playing cards inside the police department with other city officials, which brought about a general order that forbade card playing in the patrolmen's recreation room.[212] Of the sixty-three indictments handed down by the Rockingham Grand Jury in October 1911, nine were for gambling and nine others were for running disorderly houses, to include the indictments of Madam Alta Roberts and Mary Baker.[213]

Portsmouth around 1914, by unidentified artist. The painting hangs in Portsmouth City Hall. *Photo by the author.*

Officer James Kehol. *Image the property of the Portsmouth Police Department and Portsmouth Athenaeum, used with permission.*

It was clear that the community had grown tired of the rough and seedy side of Portsmouth.[214] Anger had grown toward the sailors and marines, who were blamed for ruining the quality of life for the residents with their frequent drunkenness, lust for prostitutes and love of gambling. The city council ended a long-standing tradition by announcing that the council would not allow the "bluejackets" to march in the Memorial Day Parade, a decision that greatly infuriated the navy. This order to bar the sailors and marines from marching in the parade was later reversed by the city council just in time for the sailors to march, but significant community discussion had started concerning the future vision of the downtown—one that did not include openly drunk people, frequent brawls, audacious prostitution or gambling.

The public cried out, the navy demanded a general cleanup of the downtown and Water Street areas, local elections changed the politicians and even Marshal Entwistle was pressured to resign his post, to be replaced by City Marshal Michael Hurley in 1912.[215] A tough reform team was born, made up of Mayor Daniel Badger, the police under Marshal Hurley and Mary and Josie Prescott, who would later buy up all the brothels in and

Madam Alta Warren Roberts in front of her home on Marcy Street (formerly Water Street) in 1933. *Photo the property of Kimberly Crisp, used with permission.*

around Water Street so they could tear them down to make Prescott Park. By 1913, many of the madams had been arrested, and the prostitutes were rounded up and given twenty-four hours to leave town. So ended the era of the Water Street red-light district.

EPILOGUE

The stories continue. The Roaring Twenties saw the police trying to deal with Prohibition. The bars, saloons and taverns continued underground as illegal shipments of booze arrived from Canada by truck and ship. The police were expected to run the more blatant bootleggers out of town,

1949 Portsmouth Police officers. *Image the property of the Portsmouth Police Department, used with permission.*

Portsmouth Police patch. *Scanned by author.*

while those in local favor operated under the seemingly conspiring eyes of the marshal. The world war years once again saw Portsmouth lively with drunken sailors from the shipyard and brazen prostitution, as well as investigations into the threat of spies and rumored Nazi submarines in the harbor. The civil rights movement of the '60s and '70s brought an attack on racist police officers and their headquarters, while the '80s sought reform from a thump-and-dump reputation of police brutality.

It seems fitting to write about these stories and to continue them in a second volume because the cumulative tales have a happy ending and important lessons to share. In the 2000s, Portsmouth completed a significant transformation and began to receive awards for being one of the best communities on earth, and the police department was saluted nationwide as one of the finest community policing departments.

Portsmouth is a story of hope. It was born like most cities, grew and suffered like most but matured into a magnificent place to live and visit. Leaders need only to look at Portsmouth's history to see how it can be done. The answers are within these stories. Stand by for more…

NOTES

DEDICATION

1. Mayor William H. Sise called the police officers "Guardians of our City" in his 1880 inaugural address. He would later serve as one of the first Portsmouth Police commissioners.

INDIANS AND EXILES

2. These natives were called many names to include the Piscataquas, Abenakis, Alnobaks and Algonquins, meaning "people of the dawn," "living nearest to the morning sun" or "easterners."
3. Also spelled Thompson.
4. Also called Fort Pannaway and located at present-day Odiorne Point.
5. Also called a meetinghouse—an all-purpose building that was also used for temporary lodging of the homeless.
6. Present-day Court and Marcy Streets.
7. The larger tribe Algonquins, which incorporated the Abenakis (also spelled Abnaki), numbered around 3,000, while the Abenaki tribe in and around Portsmouth had 350 natives.
8. A romantic naming of the area because of its abundance of wild strawberries along the banks. The 1653 petition to the General Court in Boston asking the area to later be renamed Portsmouth makes reference to the area's current name: "Strawbery Banke, accidentally soe called by reason of a banke where strawberries were found in this place."
9. This annexing to Massachusetts would last until 1680.
10. A place where any person could gather fresh water from a deep well. Portsmouth had a town pump in the middle of present-day Market

Square, and this was where the citizens would often hold whippings or "teasing" and hand out public punishment. Another town pump was later located at present-day Dennett Street and Maplewood Avenue.

11. Heresy is holding a belief that is contrary with church teachings. Banishment as punishment and as a means of community protection was clearly visible when the thief Henry Tufts was banished from Lee, New Hampshire, in late 1770/early 1771. A mob of drunk citizens formed at his home and began to tear it apart, board by board, until Tuft brandished a gun to cause their forced removal. The next day, Tufts wrote, "This furious attempt upon me, in my own castle, was a convincing proof, that I could no longer abide at home in peace of safety. For that reason I took leave of my family, and quitted Lee, not knowing whither to shape my course." Tufts would be the victim of a beating in Portsmouth in 1775, and his assailants would spend time in the Portsmouth Jail. Tufts wrote about an attempted crime trip to Portsmouth in 1777, when he "ventured nocturnally…in hopes of meeting with some windfall there; but discovering no prospect of that kind, I wheeled to the right about, and set off under shroud of darkness for Stratham, where I had trusty associates."

12. 1648: The first New England hanging of a person for witchcraft was in Charlestown, Massachusetts, when Margaret Jones "possessed so much malignity, that if she touched a person in anger, however slightly, it produced convulsions, or other disorders, attended with violent pains." Portsmouth would have its first witchcraft incident in 1656 with the Goodwife Walford.

Pirates

13. A small, two-masted, shallow-draft ship that could be sailed or rowed.

14. Nine very small islands located six miles off the coast of New Hampshire and Maine. It quickly grew to 1,500 fishermen living in huts made of "sod, rocks or boards and shingles brought over from the mainland." To curb prostitution, women were not allowed on the island, but this law was ignored.

15. Modern-day Bristol, in Lincoln County, Maine.

16. A small, light boat often used as a tender for larger ships. It is propelled by oars or a small sail.

Constables

17. The wives of Markwell and Roger Thomas were also ordered to leave by Constable John Snell, who was issued separate warrants in 1692.

18. Judge Sewall mentioned smallpox breaking out in Portsmouth and Exeter in 1686. There was little known about how to treat smallpox, but it was believed to have first arrived in Portsmouth via the cotton trade from the West Indies. Present-day Shapleigh Island (an island between present-day Portsmouth and New Castle) was used to quarantine those suspected of being sick or ill. Before a ship's crew or visiting travelers could enter Portsmouth, they would have to be deemed healthy and free from disease. Those ill or those suspected of being ill would have to stay on "Pest Island" until they recovered or died. There was another outbreak of smallpox in 1692.

19. Accusations and "triers" of fact were the town selectmen. It was they who would loosely arbitrate and decide what, if any, punishment would be administered. Most punishment was in the form of fines.

20. Also why the state is called "New" Hampshire.

21. In 1651, the town fathers agreed to destroy the first twenty-three years of written documents pertaining to the formation of Strawbery Banke in what many believe to be an attempt to rid Captain Mason of his claim to the area. When Strawbery Banke was renamed Portsmouth in 1653 by the Massachusetts General Assembly, a suspicious fire burned down the building near the Plains that held the remaining written records and deeds of Captain John Mason. In 1681, Sheriff James Sherlock and his deputies were brought into the area because the local constables would not evict or put an end to the political turmoil involving the resurgence of support for the Mason claim. Sheriff Sherlock ran out of town those supporting the Mason claim or removed them to the jail in New Castle.

22. The Indian name *sagamore* defines a petty Indian chief as opposed to the superior *sachem*.

23. The Mayflower Compact of 1620 recognized the English common laws in the colonies as being just and equal and was closely followed until the Revolutionary War, when the colonists rejected most things English and formed a new American legal system of written rules, free access to the courts and case law that would be guided by a constitution. Early courts did not have "professional" judges or lawyers because those qualified did not want to travel away from England and risk the dangers of the new country. Those running colonial courts had little legal training. Poorly trained magistrates ruled on issues, and juries were seldom assembled except for capital crimes. The goals of the early trials were to convince the defendant to confess and repent and then to publicly punish offenders to discourage others from breaking rules, thus restoring order. At a time when entertainment was lacking, these "trials" were often well attended, as they brought much wanted social drama to the community.

24. The term "constable" was first introduced in 1066 during the Norman invasion of England and meant a position of high prestige. Joshua

Pitts is credited in 1634 with being the first constable in America in the Plymouth Colony.

25. There are many spellings of Strawbery Banke as it is commonly spelled today, to include StrawberyBanke (one word), Strawberry Bank and variations that drop the capitalizations of the words.

26. The currency meaning of "L" here represents the pound sterling or the "pound" (each pound equals twenty shillings), the "S" represents the shilling (each shilling equals twelve pennies) and the "D" represents the penny or the pence.

WITCHES AND TITHINGMEN

27. Three men were also believed to be witches in the Strawbery Banke area. One was Thomas Turpin, who later drowned; another was called "old Ham"; and a third was nameless. On March 26, 1669, Walford won a lawsuit and recovered damages after being falsely accused of being a witch.

28. On February 19, 1693, John Westbrooke, William Cotton Being and Jon Sherborne were summoned to appear before the selectmen for cutting timber on the town's lands. In November 1697, Constable Nellson was given a warrant to bring in John Philbrook for cutting down trees, and with his confession, he was ordered to return one thousand feet of pine boards for the use of the town or pay the fine of twenty shillings. A 1691 law required all trees on common lands twenty-four inches or more in diameter to be reserved for use by the Crown.

29. Period slang name for rum.

30. Although a shilling is not used as currency today, it would be currently valued at approximately ten cents.

31. Twelve pence equals one shilling.

32. Another term for operating an illegal saloon or brothel.

33. Captain Bryan Pendleton's wife was also brought to court in 1663 for being "overtaken with drinke [sic]" and had to pay a ten-shilling fine and court costs.

34. Smoking tobacco in a posted "No Smoking" area was a five-shilling fine "for use of the Town" in 1672. Sleeping on the Sabbath was sometimes met with a day in the cage.

35. The colonists had little money to build jails or feed prisoners. Most jails were used for those who owed debts or to house people awaiting trials. Most people awaiting trails were trusted to stay at home and work until the trials or made to post cash bail. Some sentences were served in other people's homes, such as the case of the minister Moody in 1672. He was sentenced to thirteen weeks in gaol for "refusing to administer the

sacrament of the Lord's Supper according to the manner and form set forth in the book of common prayer" but actually served his time at the home of Captain Elias Stiles. At the end of his sentence, he promised not to preach again in this town and left for Boston.

36. The meetinghouse was located in the area of present-day Meeting House Hill.

37. The records in 1669 showed that two wolves were killed, and the bounty was paid out to someone not identified. Aron Moses was paid for the killing of two wolves in 1692.

38. Located at 76 Northwest Street, Portsmouth.

39. The first tavern license was issued to Henry Sherburne on March 24, 1669, for his State and Water Streets business. The first registered license in Portsmouth to brew and sell "beare" was granted to Samuel Wentworth in 1670.

40. Present-day Fort Constitution at New Castle.

41. External protection from the Indians was often provided by local militia.

42. Also spelled tythingmen and tithing-man.

43. Examples of Sabbath rules were no working, no traveling, no loafing around taverns and paying attention in church.

44. This system is mentioned in the Pentateuch (Torah) and can be traced back as far as Moses, who used it to help govern Israel.

45. The office of the modern-day sheriff is derived from the shire-reeve and is the oldest law enforcement position in the United States.

46. This originated from twelfth-century England, when certain knights were appointed by King Richard I to keep the peace. In 1631, the justice of the peace held police, judicial and administrative authority within the community. By the 1900s, these powers had been significantly reduced and divided among judges, the police and locally elected officials.

47. *Posse comitatus* translates literally to mean "force of the country."

48. This concept required neighbors to band together and assist one another in times of trouble or to pursue fleeing criminals and predates the Norman conquest of 1066. It was understood that everyone would join in the chase of a felon once the hue and cry was put out.

49. "Qua" and "qua keeper" were colonial-day slang words for jail and jail keeper. To "crack the qua" meant you had escaped from jail. Prisoners were also called "drag."

50. Common punishment for debtors was jail; however, the problem was getting them to pay off their debts during the time they were jailed and not working. In 1739, Sam Bathrick was placed in the Chestnut Street jail for being a debtor. Six years later, he still sat in jail because he still owed money. A petition was circulated by the townspeople demanding that he be released from jail so that he could work off his debt—how else could

he pay back those he owed if he was not allowed to work? The legislature decided to charge those he owed five shillings a week to hold Bathrick in jail. If they did not pay, Bathrick would be released and forced to serve in the military at Fort William and Mary (present-day Fort Constitution in New Castle), with half his pay going to pay off the debts. It is not known what happened to Sam Bathrick, but New Hampshire outlawed imprisoning debtors in 1840.

51. This would happen again in 1750, when Sheriff Edward Hart served a debtor's writ on General Nathaniel Peabody that read, "Money, jail, or bail." Peabody asked the sheriff to let him go (temporarily) free to allow him time to turn himself into the Exeter Jail because it would be closer to his home and easier and more convenient for Peabody to work out the particulars for his release. Sheriff Hart consented, but Peabody failed to turn himself in and became a fugitive. Hart was then ordered liable for Peabody's debts. Sheriff Hart had two friends (Judge John Pickering and Dr. William Cutter) who paid off the debts for Sheriff Hart. Sheriff Hart repaid them later by seizing some of Peabody's land and selling it.

CHAOS AND ORDER

52. Another name for the privately run poorhouse and sometimes used as a jail to house nonviolent people. Portsmouth claims to have the country's first public "pauper workhouse," which was voted to be built on April 9, 1711, and was in operation by 1716 at the corner of present-day Chestnut and Porter Streets. It would be abandoned in 1755, when a newer one was built on Court Street.

53. Some accounts have Walton's neighbor, Hannah Jones, as the accused witch.

54. Led by Chiefs Kancamagus and Mesandowit.

55. The most northern point of land that separates Great Bay from Little Bay in present-day Newington.

56. The present-day Wentworth by the Sea golf course area of Rye, New Hampshire.

57. The year 1693 also represents a landmark moment in police history when officers of New York City donned the first police uniform.

58. The Treaty of Pemaquid.

59. New Castle was incorporated on May 30, 1693.

60. Also known as the first French and Indian Wars, these battles with the Indians, who were supported and sometimes led by the French in Canada, lasted nine years (1688–97). The Treaty of Ryswick in 1697 formally ended hostilities between the French and English. Raids on the

English settlers significantly diminished without the French instigating and supporting the Indians to attack.

61. Present-day Durham, New Hampshire.

62. "Pulpit" farm was situated about two miles north of downtown, at present-day Spinnaker Point and Osprey Landing.

63. In 1693, there were 270 names logged at the old meetinghouse in the South End. These names did not include unmarried adults or children. This Indian attack would have depleted approximately one-third of the population of Portsmouth.

64. Those captured were never returned, and their fates remain unknown.

65. Another account had her entire hands being removed "because the Indians could not immediately remove the rings off her fingers."

66. The Plains is on the remote outskirts of town, nearly two miles from the downtown waterfront area, and contained several large farms and the famous Plains Tavern (saloon). It would later serve as the local militia training field and muster grounds. Portsmouth Plains is located in the area of Islington Street and Greenland Road and is the current home of the Little League baseball field. The first baseball game played there was in 1866, when Concord beat Portsmouth 31–26.

67. Mary Brewster was found alive but scalped by a tomahawk. She survived, later had four sons and would live to the age of seventy-eight.

68. The area of Strawbery Banke and the Puddle Dock was the center of town in 1700.

69. Five houses and nine barns, including stabled cattle, hogs, one horse, grains and hay, were destroyed in these fires.

70. This one measured twelve feet square, with stocks inside and a pillory located on top.

71. The most likely area of the jail was between what is now Fleet Street and the North Church.

72. Colonial-day slang for gallows was "nippin jig."

73. Dried codfish could last anywhere from three to ten years without spoiling.

74. *Quintal* is Latin for hundred-like, so one quintal equals approximately one hundred of something; in the case of measuring the production of fish, one quintal would equal about one hundred pounds of fish.

75. Prisons differ from jails because jails are used for pre-trial and minor crime confinement while prisons are used for post-trial confinement and serving out felony or major sentences. Portsmouth had both a jail and a prison in the area of Market Square in 1700.

76. One of the unique changes the colonists made to the English form of justice was to establish a legal system that allowed the accused to be represented by counsel during court proceedings. By 1730, defendants

were allowed to have defense attorneys in criminal courts. By 1750, criminal courts were using a form of due process to protect the rights of the accused and adopted the standard of "innocent until proven guilty."

77. Most colonial criminals were men (95 percent of violent crimes and 74 percent of thefts), while women were the ones most accused of being witches.

78. Captain Robert Almory of the sloop *Hawk* was quarantined for smallpox in 1718 on Partridge Island (present-day Peirce Island), where there was already a pesthouse built by the community. Later, in 1736, there were ninety-nine people who died from an unknown virus. Eighty-one of the dead were children under ten years old.

79. Located at the corner of Court and Washington Streets and built in 1730.

80. Jaffrey lived on Middle Road about one mile from the center of town.

INFANTICIDE

81. Another means of abortion, though less popular, was to ingest herbs that would bring about a miscarriage. Often these herbs, such as pennyroyal, would be harmful, sometimes fatal, to the mother.

82. Sheriff Packer lived on the corner of State and Court Streets, which was the place where the townspeople, in 1768, would hang him in effigy for the hanging of Ruth Blay.

83. Present-day South Unitarian Universalist Church, located at 292 State Street, Portsmouth.

84. The register of probate Richard Waldron III's house in the Plains burned down in 1745, and with it went many early records of Portsmouth.

85. Present-day St. John's Church at 105 Chapel Street, Portsmouth.

86. The place where the community would keep stray or unclaimed animals.

87. The use of gallows or dropping people from high places via trapdoors in order to break their necks was not common in America until the 1870s.

88. Female prisoners often tried to look their best on hanging day. They would often have new dresses bought for them if they could afford them, or new dresses would be made by the townsfolk and given to them.

89. The term "turned off the back of the cart" refers to the action of a person standing on a cart directly under the hanging tree with the cart being driven away, leaving the person to hang.

90. About 1754, Portsmouth installed its first gas streetlights.

91. Shortly after midnight on November 18, 1755, a violent earthquake woke the townspeople, threw dishes to the floor and pewter from the dressers and even woke the sailors who were asleep on docked ships. The

shaking was so severe that some people thought it was the end of the world. Aftershocks continued for a week.

92. The newspaper was called the *New Hampshire Gazette and Historical Chronicle* and continues today as New Hampshire's oldest newspaper. The first printing was on October 7, 1756.

93. Built in 1758 in present-day Market Square (called "The Parade" in the eighteenth century) and dismantled in 1836. One-third of the building was used to construct a house on Court Street with an additional 480 pieces of major framing timbers, floorboards and sheathing; it is preserved today by the State of New Hampshire in a storage trailer in Concord.

94. Then called Spring Market. The original market square or place where people would go and buy goods was called Spring Hill or Spring Market and was located in the area of Bow, Ceres and Market Streets. Present-day Market Square was not named as such until 1838.

95. Present-day Boscawen, New Hampshire.

96. The first royal colonial governor of New Hampshire.

97. Guy Fawkes was an Englishman sentenced to be hanged on November 5, 1605, for his role in the plot to assassinate King James I and restore a Catholic monarch to the throne of England. He has been celebrated to this day by some who are opposed to England being Protestant.

98. They are also credited with organizing the first mounted police patrols in 1758.

99. This concept of preventative patrols and the theory behind its deterrence effect was emphasized in a pamphlet by Sir John Fielding, published in 1753, titled *An Account of the Origins and Effects of a Police Set on Foot by His Grace the Duke of Newcastle in the Year 1753*. He also wrote a book in 1758 titled *Plan for Preventing Robberies within Twenty Miles of London* as a study on the effectiveness of a regular force of men set on horseback patrols.

100. The origin of the term billy club comes from this pairing of a short mace outfitted to hold rolled-up warrants.

101. The house was located somewhere in the area of present-day Ward's Corner.

102. Ward's Corner is the present-day intersection of Lafayette Road and South Street, called such because the Ward family had a big house there where the Professional Park stands today. The location of the hanging is described as "about fifty feet east of the Pound which was at South and Middle."

103. Present-day Porter Street. This jail was located at the site of the present-day Music Hall on Chestnut Street.

104. Less than ten years later, in 1766, this Chestnut Street jail would need work to make it more secure. The town allocated £119 to fix the jail so that prisoners, mostly made up of debtors, could not escape.

105. Site of the present-day Rockingham Hotel.
106. Located on Fetter Street or present-day Porter Street in the area of the Music Hall.
107. The town pump was in front of the statehouse and North Church, east toward Daniel Street, in present-day Market Square. It consisted of a freshwater well with a hand pump that would draw drinking water into a trough for horses and other animals.
108. A hostler is a person who tends to horses in a stable.
109. One gate was specifically built on Post Road, or today's Greenland Road, in the area of Interstate 95.
110. Most likely these "armed guards" were militia and not the constables.
111. Called in short the Stamp Act of 1765 because printed documents such as legal papers, newspapers and such could be printed only on paper produced in England that bore a special revenue stamp. Two years later, the Townshend Act of 1767 required all colonists to pay personal taxes to the Crown and further inflamed the colonists.
112. Present-day Court and Middle Streets, though some accounts had the mock funeral at the jail on Prison Lane (Chestnut and Porter Streets).
113. Approximately 124 males and 63 females.
114. A slave of Colonel William Brewster.
115. Prince Jackson was later arrested for another theft, this one being heard in the white county court. He was found guilty of this theft, but the outcome of these charges is not known.

HANGINGS AND AN UNSOLVED MURDER

116. The law against infanticide was repealed in 1793.
117. Present-day Danville, New Hampshire.
118. Dr. Josiah Bartlett, one of the signers of the Declaration of Independence eight years later, was the doctor assigned to treat Ruth Blay.
119. Present-day Chestnut Street.
120. This would also serve as the first New Hampshire Statehouse following the Revolution, with the name of King Street later changed to Congress Street.
121. Present-day South Cemetery in the section called Proprietors' Burial Ground. The land then was mostly used as pasture and as a training grounds for the military. It would not be used as a cemetery until 1830.
122. Located at State and Court Streets. Following Sheriff Packard's death in 1771, the house became Colonel Brewster's Tavern, at which President George Washington was later thought to have stayed for four nights.
123. Today, it is much the opposite, with the Portsmouth Police being responsible for the criminal investigation of all felonies, misdemeanors

and violations, while the county sheriff has jurisdiction on mostly civil processes such as evictions and lawsuit notifications.

124. Samuel Chandler, an apprentice of barber Peter Mann, was suspected and arrested for the burglaries of Mr. Cutts's dry goods store, Mr. Penhallow's wares store and Mr. Griffith's watch store. Chandler confessed his crimes, and the stolen merchandise was found in the attic of the statehouse. Chandler was banished from the town, a punishment typical of those who confessed early on in an investigation.

125. Frenchman's Lane got its name because of the October 23, 1778 robbery and murder of Frenchman John Dustin along the "quiet country path at the Creek." He was between the ages of twenty-five and thirty-five and was found shortly before dawn by a neighbor. Dustin's head was half severed, and the investigation suggested he was killed by two men who were never identified. Benjamin P. Shillaber wrote this poem of the murder: "Most lovely the spot, yet dark was the tale; / That made the red lips of boyhood pale, / Of the Frenchman's doom and the bitter strife, / Of the blood stained sword and the gleaming knife, / Of the gory rock set the wrong to speak, / In Frenchman's Lane, up by Islington Creek."

126. Fort William and Mary was constructed from 1666 until completion in 1694. Today, it is called Fort Constitution, but under the moonlit night of December 14, 1774, the colonists of Portsmouth, led by Major John Sullivan, arrived at what was then called Fort William and Mary. They traveled by gundalow (a small, shallow-berth barge used to move goods up and down the Piscataqua River to Dover, Durham and Exeter) from Portsmouth and captured the thinly defended fort. Captain John Cochran and five soldiers surrendered the king's colors quickly and without a shot being fired. About one hundred barrels of gunpowder, two dozen light cannons and many small arms were removed and later brought to the Battle of Bunker Hill. It is said that the "shot heard 'round the world" (on April 19, 1775, in Lexington and Concord, Massachusetts)—and the first official overt military actions against England—was fired with powder seized by the Portsmouth colonists.

127. On December 13, 1774, Paul Revere would mark the first of his many visits to the colonies when he arrived at Stoodley's Tavern on Daniel Street to deliver a letter to Captain Samuel Cutts. This letter was from the Boston Patriots, who were warning the Portsmouth Patriots that the British were coming with shiploads of troops to reinforce Fort William and Mary. This warning would be the final catalyst needed for the colonists' attack on Fort William and Mary just one day later.

128. Formally called King Street.

129. It's unknown if this total included the 140 slaves.

130. One of the major preparations was the building of Fort Washington in 1775 on present-day Peirce Island to protect the harbor and the

downtown area of Portsmouth. The other major construction was of the frigate *Raleigh*. It was outfitted with thirty-two guns and launched on May 21, 1776. This ship is depicted on the present-day shoulder patch worn by all uniformed Portsmouth Police officers and forms the centerpiece of the New Hampshire state seal.

A MODEL POLICE FORCE

131. Exeter was the capital of New Hampshire until 1808, when Concord was named (and currently maintains this role) state capital.
132. By 1799, Portsmouth was the twelfth-largest city in the United States with 5,339 people.
133. Infrastructure improvements included water pipes running underground for nearly three miles through hollowed-out wooden logs from the well at Oak Hill Farm or the area of the present-day Harvard Street pumping station to downtown, where the Portsmouth Aqueduct Company supplied the water for 214 houses and stores. The fresh water was necessary to help quell dysentery, which had recently killed fifty-two people in the South End, and yellow fever, which had killed fifty-five people in the North End. Armed guards were used to quarantine the area around the ship *Mentor*, which was tied up at the Sheafe Wharf when its sailors were suspected of being the carrier of the local yellow fever epidemic when two of them first showed signs of the sickness. The ship had just arrived with a load of sugar, molasses and coffee from the French Caribbean island Martinique, where yellow fever was prevalent. At night, you could hear the undertaker calling out, "Bring out your dead!" as those who had perished during the day were gathered up and buried in the North Cemetery.
134. The great fire of 1802 started inside this bank.
135. The first great fire started on December 26, 1802, and lasted a full day. It destroyed 114 houses and stores and caused over $200,000 in damage. This devastating urban fire was widely seen as the first declared national disaster and brought about approval from the U.S. Congress to use federal resources and money to help Portsmouth recover. There was another large fire in 1806, costing the town $70,000, and a great fire in 1813, during which 272 buildings burned, costing the city $300,000. Approximately 130 families were displaced from 108 dwellings; 64 stores and shops burned, along with 100 barns. The only thing that stopped the fire from destroying the whole downtown was the wind blowing the fire toward the Piscataqua River, which formed an effective firebreak. The last nineteenth-century great fire in Portsmouth was in 1864, when 15 downtown buildings were destroyed.

136. Established on June 17, 1800, under President Thomas Jefferson, it continues to be the oldest running shipyard of the United States.

137. He would call his years in Portsmouth (1807–16) "the best years" of his life.

138. The law against concealing the death of a newborn was repealed in 1793. Since 1608, there have been over fifteen thousand executions in the United States for offenses such as concealing the death of a newborn, horse theft and murder.

139. One distinct difference between a constable and a police officer is that a police officer may arrest without a warrant in limited circumstances. The police officer could also have direct access to the courts by filing a complaint that outlined the criminal allegation. A constable was allowed to arrest only with a magistrate's warrant, and it was the issuing magistrate who had access to the court.

140. Market Square got its name in 1800, when the new brick market was built. Measuring eighty feet by thirty-five feet, it was supported by sixteen arches, which made the inside unobstructed by support poles. When completed in September, the building represented the official movement of downtown from the waterfront area.

141. The Portsmouth Bathhouse lasted close to a century because most people could not afford bathtubs in their homes.

142. The practice of whipping and branding would not be outlawed in New Hampshire until 1829. Branding was a painful form of tattooing where a piece of cork with several needles projecting from it would be dipped into India ink and then used to mark the words issued by the court on the face of the prisoner. The prisoner was not permitted to disturb the ink or the protruding blood in any way until it had the chance to dry completely. The common tool used for whipping was the cat o' nine tails with a wire knot tied at the end. Sometimes to add to the pain, salt water was used to clean the wounds.

143. Charles Brewster, author of *Brewster's Rambles about Portsmouth*, wrote of the jail, "Our residence being next door to the Jail, our young blood was often chilled by the frequent exhibition of clotted gore on the bare backs of naked culprits, who were tied up to the public whipping post, or pinioned on the jail door for branding."

144. It also served as the public library.

145. Present-day Court Street between Fleet and Pleasant Streets.

146. He served from 1801 to 1825.

147. Loose dogs were kept at the town pound, and when the owners came to pick them up, they were given a warning that the next time the dog was caught loose, the dog would face the same penalty as one who would tear down the flag—which was death.

148. Grog is a mixture of rum and water often flavored with lemon, sugar and spices. It is often served hot.

149. A privateer is a private person or privately owned shipping company authorized by the government to attack and capture enemy ships during wartime. In the War of 1812, Portsmouth had over fourteen of these fast and low-profile privateers, which quickly sold their prizes in Portsmouth and split their bounty among the sailors who sailed on board and the owner(s) of the ship. Captain George Fishley is perhaps one of native Portsmouth's most famous privateers; he took up this profession after serving in the Revolutionary War, fighting at the Battles of Monmouth and Valley Forge. He fought in Valley Forge without his "shoes or stockings," according to his obituary.

150. In 1761, Wyseman Clagett was fined for using profane language after he sent one of his servants to "insult the owner" of a disputed load of wood for sale.

151. There were also 1,453 sailors and 581 fishermen (fishing cod, pollack and mackerel) working in and out of Portsmouth who were not counted as inhabitants.

152. It opened on State Street in 1833.

A POLICE DEPARTMENT IS BORN

153. The New York City Police Department was officially formed in 1844, but it would not be until 1898 that New York City centralized all of its eighteen individual police departments (now called precincts) into the one department it is today.

154. Other police agencies formed in 1850 include the Los Angeles Police, the Pinkerton Detective Agency and the Wells Fargo detective bureau.

155. The mayor had considerable influence over the city marshal and frequently replaced him. The mayor also used his position to control the police officers under the marshal, whereby, in 1865, it was clarified by ordinance that it would be the marshal and only the marshal who could give orders to the officers, and the officers would be held accountable only to the marshal.

156. The development of the railroad was important for local industry. Cities like Manchester and Concord had overtaken Portsmouth's textile business because of their access to the Merrimack River for water power, the availability of cheap immigrant labor and the development of the eastern railroad to transport raw materials into the factories and transport the completed products out along the East Coast.

157. The gold rush in California and the China trade spurred the need for fast, sleek ships to transport people and goods to the West Coast. The

clipper ships were the fastest known ships at the time, and the railroad was not yet developed to transport goods all the way west to the Pacific coast. Some of the world's fastest clipper ships were built in Portsmouth during the 1840s and 1850s. The ship *Typhoon*, built at Badgers Island, set a world record on March 13, 1851, when it sailed from Portsmouth to Liverpool, England, in just thirteen days.

158. The majority of city ordinances in 1850 pertained to health issues such as the disposal of dead animals, the need to quarantine sick people before they were allowed ashore and the disposal of wastewater to combat smallpox and dysentery. It would have been appropriate for all city officials, including the city marshal, to be given orders to be on the watch for these issues and to report them to the appropriate city health official.

159. On March 10, 1853, the Concord Police Department was formed, with tax collecting being one of the official duties of the city marshal.

160. Portsmouth policemen were all required to wear their assigned badges while on duty, but uniforms were not yet required. The city marshal, on June 16, 1853, was required to wear a cockade or a knot of ribbons with bright colors on his hat to distinguish his office. The assistant marshal was required to wear a star on the left lapel of his coat.

161. The first police department in the United States to merge both day and night watch into a single police department was the New York City Police in 1844.

Rogues and Questionable Characters

162. White's Road was later renamed Spinney Road in memoriam of Sarah Spinney.

163. According to the U.S. Census Bureau website, the population in Portsmouth for 2010 was 20,779 total inhabitants. The total number of arrests in 2010 was 1,242, or approximately 6 percent of the city's population, excluding visitors or nonresidents.

164. "Watchman" is a word used commonly to refer to the police officers who work the overnight shifts or midnight shifts. The captain of the watch would be the person in charge of the midnight shift.

165. Soldiers such as those in Company K used the banks of the South Millpond to practice formations and military movements. Company K would ship out on June 2, 1861, to fight in the Battle of Bull Run.

166. Portsmouth city council approved an additional $100 to $300 to be given to each Portsmouth citizen who answered the draft or enlisted in support of the president's call for an army of 300,000 men to fight in the Civil War.

167. The New York City Draft Riots were suppressed only with the military using great force, including artillery and fixed bayonets, on the mostly middle-class New Yorkers who rioted. A total of 50,000 to 75,000 people were involved, and in the end, there were dead bodies set on fire or left hanging from lampposts, an orphanage for black children was set on fire and up to 350 people were dead and 2,000 wounded. This event was the focus of the 2002 movie *Gangs of New York* starring Leonardo DiCaprio.

168. It was also reported that they merely wanted him to hang a U.S. flag, but he ran off when he realized he did not have one on the property.

169. The Thames River Police in England in 1798 is credited with being the first police force to wear uniforms. The English Metropolitan Police Act in 1829 required the police to wear blue uniforms to set them apart from the scarlet-colored military uniforms. The New York Police in 1844 (called the Harper's Police at the time—named after the mayor who formed them) would be the first department in the United States to wear uniforms. Twenty-one years later, the Portsmouth Police would require blue uniforms to be worn, with badges carried by all police officers on duty. The wearing of uniforms in Portsmouth and other places was a haphazard occurrence up to this point, with many officers wearing their personal shirts or coats with badges pinned on their chests.

170. The marshal was required every three months to provide a report on the police department to the mayor.

171. It was not only the police who used these "rattles" to call for help; an elderly resident living in the Warner House in 1888 used a wooden policeman's rattle to summon a nearby police officer about an intruder in the house.

172. City Marshal J. Horace Kent left the police department to serve with the United States Secret Service, which had been formed a few months earlier, on July 5, 1865, to suppress the producers of counterfeited money that had become the source of nearly one-third of all U.S. currency in circulation. It would not be until the assassination of President McKinley in 1901 that the Secret Service would be charged with the protection of the president. Agent Kent served in the Secret Service until 1871, when he returned to Portsmouth to once again serve as city marshal. In 1876, he became sheriff of Rockingham County until 1887, when he lost the election but became warden of the state prison.

173. The word "copper" was first used in print in the February 21, 1846 edition of the *National Police Gazette*.

174. Portsmouth would install its first street call light system in 1890. The lights were located on the Creek beat, at the upper end of Market Street and on Water Street.

175. Known as the "Turf Fraud Scandal" or the "Trial of the Detectives."
176. In 1890, the marshal reported that he did not have enough police badges to go around and that the guns used were the size of "gatling guns" or the same quality and effectiveness as a Fourth of July shooter. He also asked that the police no longer be tasked with extinguishing the gas streetlights "because it is easy for any evil disposed person to watch when the officer makes his rounds at eleven o'clock; which is the hour designated for turning off the lights; to follow the officer as he extinguishes them, and thus learn the exact locality and route he follows night after night."

The Murder of Prisoner Canty by Officer Smith

177. Cities such as New York were riddled with voter fraud at this time. It was not uncommon for political parties to pay citizens to vote for their party or for a voter to vote early in the morning wearing a beard, cast another ballot later in the morning after shaving his beard and entering with just a mustache and then vote again later in the afternoon, after shaving a third time, all to conceal his true identity and to gain multiple votes by the same voter for a desired candidate. There were also instances where one political party would quasi kidnap immigrants using violence or intimidation to coerce him to vote for a certain candidate.
178. The police department was allocated $566 in 1877 to pay for extra and auxiliary police services. Officer Smith was a carpenter by trade who lived at 10 Myrtle Street. He served as a part-time auxiliary police officer.
179. Daniel E. Ayers's Store was located at 15 North Road, between the North Mill Bridge and Cutts. It sold groceries.
180. Twisters were a type of handcuff that consisted of a short chain with an interlocking metal handle at each end. The chain would be placed around the wrist and the handles brought together into the hand of the police officer. The chain, now securely wrapped around the wrist of a prisoner, could be twisted by the officer holding the handles, inflicting great pain to the wrist area of the prisoner. This device proved useful, not only in gaining the compliance of an aggressive person, but also in helping to control and hold one arm of the prisoner.
181. The police station was headquartered in Market Square at the Brick Market, along with the other city offices.
182. In the area of North and Dearborn Streets, or "two or three minutes" away from Ayers's Store. (*Portsmouth Daily Chronicle*, March 17, 1876.)

183. Testimony from bystander James McGraw offered that there were at least four blows delivered to Canty's head by Officer Smith. Testimony from Reverend Lot L. Harmen, who was walking near the officers, stated he saw Canty get out of the twisters and fight with the officers. Harmen thought there were as many as six blows delivered to Canty's head by Officer Smith's billy club.

184. Godfrey Canty was a laborer by trade and lived on Cate Street.

185. The first and only ballot came back with eleven jurors finding Smith "acquitted" and one juror finding him "not guilty of manslaughter but blamable of simple assault."

DRUNKEN COPS AND THE POLICE COMMISSION

186. Most "neglect of duty" charges began with an officer being either drunk or asleep at his post. When a patrol officer was caught drinking or sleeping on duty, the police commission would often suspend the officer for the act and his commanding officer for neglect of duty because of improper supervision.

187. City Marshal Entwistle asked for and received the resignations of Officers Jacob B. Burnes and Dennis Murphy upon completion of these suspensions.

188. Only six of the twenty-five men would survive the three-year Arctic expedition that started in 1881 and ended in 1884.

189. This naval prison, also called the "Alcatraz of the East," would be occupied with more than eighty-six thousand navy and marine inmates from 1908 until its closure in 1974. The 1973 movie *The Last Detail*, starring Jack Nicholson and Randy Quaid, was based on a prisoner transport story to the Portsmouth Naval Prison, called in the movie "the worst place on earth." Several scenes were shot on the actual site of the prison. It still stands today but shows the effects of forty years of neglect and decay

190. The officers were also given ten sick days per year and 100 percent of their pay during their convalescence should they become injured on duty.

191. $2.50 a day in 1895 is equal to $65.90 in 2009, according to the salary consumer price index equivalency chart.

192. $1,000 a year is equal to $26,400 in 2009, according to the salary consumer price index equivalency chart.

193. The Rockingham County Courthouse was located on State Street between Pleasant and Penhallow Streets. It was later torn down because it needed repairs that were too costly at the time. There is now a bank parking lot where this building once stood.

194. A bobbin boy was common labor among the youth at that time. They would keep the women working the textile looms supplied with full

bobbins loaded with cotton or wool thread. Pay was about $1.00 to $1.20 per week.

195. Located in Andersonville, Georgia, the twenty-seven-acre open-air prison was used for only fourteen months. The men lived in tents because barracks were never built. The men were contained by walls made of pine logs standing twenty feet upright from the ground. Andersonville Prison was designed to hold ten thousand men but would often hold upward of thirty-three thousand men at any one time. More than forty-five thousand Union soldiers were confined there, with almost thirteen thousand of them dying from disease, poor sanitation, malnutrition, overcrowding or exposure to the elements.

196. On March 6, 1873, Karen and Anethe Christensen were brutally murdered on Smuttynose Island at the Isle of Shoals. Maren Hontvet barely escaped being murdered by hiding on the other side of the island. She became a key witness and identified German fisherman Louis Wagner as the man who had strangled one and bludgeoned the other with an axe. Wagner escaped to Boston but was brought back to Portsmouth by City Marshal Frank B. Johnson and Entwistle and was greeted by thousands of residents shouting their disdain for Wagner, yelling, "Hang him!" while others threw stones. He would spend that night in the Portsmouth jail, but the trial was conducted in Saco, Maine, because Smuttynose Island is in the state of Maine and it had jurisdiction. Wagner asserted his innocence but would be found guilty after a nine-day trial and later hanged on June 5, 1875. There have been several books printed (*Moonlight Murder at Smuttynose* by Lyman V. Rutledge, *Return to Smuttynose Island* by Emeric Spooner, *Cold Water Crossing* by David Faxon and *The Weight of Water* by Anita Shreve), along with one major movie, titled *The Weight of Water*, featuring actors Elizabeth Hurley and Sean Penn—all presenting evidence that Wagner might have been innocent. Some modern alternate theories suggest that Maren Hontvet killed them for their possessions or perhaps killed them after she found Karen and Anethe involved in a lurid love encounter and identified Wagner as the murderer to cover her tracks. Yet another theory is that Maren's husband killed them and Maren identified Wagner to cover for her husband.

197. The Warwick continues to operate today as a private men-only club and is located on Market Street at the corner of Daniel Street on the third floor above Alie Jewelry.

198. The padded cell was installed at the jail in 1893 to confine "insane persons." This death investigation was cleared when the coroner ruled the death to be a heart attack brought on by excessive use of alcohol. The Rockingham County Jail on Penhallow Street would house fifty-eight prisoners in 1893. It would have no more than twenty-three at any one time, with four of these prisoners being women.

199. Present-day Marcy Street.

HOOKERS OF THE BOWERY

200. He was the largest manufacturer of beer in the United States.

201. Charles Walker owned the coal docks at the end of State Street and would use his ferry to transport the sailors from the shipyard to the coal docks, which was right across the street from Mary Baker's Glouster House. Oftentimes, Madam Alta's girls could be seen waiting to greet the sailors when the ferry arrived.

202. There were as many as eleven drinking saloons on Water Street, along with the numerous bawdyhouses. Places like the Oyster Saloon, Jefferson House Saloon, the Mariner's House and the Union House Saloon might have had some soliciting prostitutes, but they lacked the boardinghouse rooms that the brothels had in which to provide space for private sex.

203. Not all bordellos were located on Water Street. On Maplewood Avenue, Hannah McSweeny operated the Commercial House, while Eva White's Elm House was on State Street. However, the most popular were located on Water Street, including Mattie Bond's Clifton House (once owned by police officer James Kehoe, who operated it as a saloon), Harry Bullard's The Home, Charles "Cappy" Stewart's house at 51 Water Street, the Glouster House and Alta Roberts's house.

204. This small island of about three hundred feet, separated from present-day Peirce Island, is today connected to Peirce by a stone and gravel causeway.

205. This quote is from the *Portsmouth Herald* and Melanie Asmar, who writes a small local newsletter.

206. Prostitutes generally charged two dollars: one dollar for the house and the other for the girl. A full night was ten dollars. The girls also got a percentage of the liquor sales.

207. Other crimes reported in 1897 ranged from an attempted sexual assault at the Haven School Yard to an accidental shooting while out hunting. Others reported in the *Portsmouth Herald* were: "Residence of Mark Noble was broken into and a fire lighted and coffee made and general edibles eaten"; "Jack Holland, in order to escape arrest for breaking glass, assault and indecent exposure, went up an elpole on Linden St. and remained there about 2 hours in a cold storm"; "Police Officer Hurley raised a sunken schooner at the Shoals"; and "Louise F. Dame arrested for stealing two cannon from the armory of Co. A. sent to jail in default of $400 bond in each case." Additionally, hundreds of counterfeit silver certificates "made things lively at local banks."

208. From 1893 to 1898, the police averaged only two arrests a year for prostitution-related crimes.

209. Patrolman Charles Quinn did not take bribes along the waterfront, and his attempts to enforce the laws grew irritating to those operating the

brothels. One night, as he made his rounds, some thugs beat him, stripped him of his uniform, pinned the flaps of his long johns with his badge and handcuffed him to the utility pole near 51 Water Street. Marshal Entwistle was called to come "get his boy." The caller suggested that Quinn be transferred to another beat or risk being found in the river. Quinn was made sergeant shortly thereafter and was put under orders to stay away from Water Street. Patrolman Michael Kelly took over the beat, and quiet again prevailed along the waterfront.

210. It is not clear if Rossi was placed in handcuffs while Murphy first escorted him to jail.

211. Standard-issue equipment for the police officer included a belt, billy club, revolver, revolver case, pair of twisters, handcuffs, badge and whistle.

212. The police department in 1911 was located on the second floor of city hall.

213. Other Portsmouth indictments included numerous burglaries, thefts, adulteries and fornications and one rape.

214. This progressive era around the country, spurred on by industrialization, urbanization and immigration, brought with it anti-prostitution and temperance. Locally, the North Church's Reverend Lucius H. Thayer and organizations such as the Woman's Christian Temperance Union and the Women's Civic League led the movement to shut down Portsmouth's red-light district.

215. After thirty-four years as a Portsmouth Police officer, twenty-four of them as city marshal, Entwistle would retire after also serving as New Hampshire senator.

BIBLIOGRAPHY

An Act to Prevent the Destroying and Murdering of Bastard Children. Portsmouth, NH: Daniel Fowle, 1761.

Adams, Nathaniel. *Annals of Portsmouth, Comprising a Period of Two Hundred Years from the First Settlement of the Town; with Biographical Sketches of a Few of the Most Respectable Inhabitants.* Exeter, NH: C. Norris, 1825.

Adams, Richard. "Lecture—Frank Jones: The Man Behind the Myths." *Portsmouth Athenaeum Lecture Series.* Portsmouth, NH: Richard Adams, 2010.

Aldrich, Thomas Bailey. *An Old Town by the Sea.* Boston: Houghton Mifflin Company, 1883. Reprint, New York, 1893.

Asmar, Melanie. "Fun Facts about Portsmouth." *Portsmouth Herald,* March 7, 2004.

Baker, Emerson W. *The Devil of Great Island.* New York: Palgrave MacMillan, 2007.

Before the Lake Was Champlain: An Untold Story of Ice Age America. Directed by Ted Timreck. Hidden Landscapes Video, 2009.

Bennett, Helen Pearson, and Harold Hotchkiss. *Vignettes of Portsmouth.* Portsmouth, NH: Stetson Press, 1913.

Bennett, James H. *Colonial Life in New Hampshire.* Chesterville, NH: Kellscraft Studio, 1899. Reprint, 2010.

Boone, Nicholas. *The Constables Pocket-Book, or, A Dialgue between an Old Constable and a New.* Boston: self-published, 1710.

Boston, City of. "A Brief History of the Boston Police Department." 2011. City of Boston.gov. http://www.cityofboston.gov/police/about/history. asp (accessed May 1, 2011).

Boston Weekly Post-Boy, August 20, 1739.

Brewster, Charles W. *Rambles about Portsmouth.* Portsmouth, NH: C.W. Brewster and Son, 1859.

BIBLIOGRAPHY

———. *Rambles about Portsmouth.* 2ⁿᵈ edition. Portsmouth, NH: Lewis W. Brewster, Portsmouth Journal Office, 1869.

Brighton, Raymond A. *They Came to Fish.* Portsmouth, NH: Peter E. Randall, 1994.

Bundles, A'Lelia. "The Power of a Dream." *Portsmouth Discover,* May 4, 2013.

Candee, Richard M. *Building Portsmouth.* Portsmouth, NH: Back Channel Press, 2006.

———. "Social Conflict and Urban Rebuilding—The Portsmouth, New Hampshire, Brick Act of 1814." *Winterthur Portfolio* 32, nos. 2/3 (Summer/Autumn 1997): 119–46.

City Clerk Log of 1850–1874. Portsmouth, NH: City of Portsmouth, 1850–1874.

Clark, Charles E. *The Eastern Frontier: The Settlement of Northern New England, 1610–1763.* New York: Alfred A. Knopf, 1970.

Cledonian Mercury. "Dreadful Riot in London." May 16, 1833.

"Colonial Period: Crime and Punishment." ENotes.com. http://www.enotes.com/crime-criminals-almanac/colonial-period (accessed January 22, 2011).

Colquhoun, Patrick. *Treatise on the Commerce and Police of the River Thames.* New York: Harper and Bros., 1846.

Committee, City of Portsmouth 350ᵗʰ Anniversary. "Celebrating the 350ᵗʰ Anniversary of the First Settlement in New Hampshire and the Founding of Our State, Portsmouth, New Hampshire." *Portsmouth 350 from 1623–1973.* Portsmouth, NH: Ranger Publications, Inc., 1973.

Conner, C.G., clerk of Rockingham Superior Court. *Subpoena Order for Witness in the Case of State v. Andrew J. Smith.* Subpoena. Retrieved from the NH Division of Archives and Records Management. Exeter, NH: Rockingham County Superior Court, 1876.

Coroner's Inquiry, March 16, 1876. *Complaint upon Andrew J. Smith.* Complaint. Rockingham County, NH, 1876.

Costello, A.E. *History of the New Haven Police Department (1892): from the Period of the Old Watch in Colonial Days to the Present Time.* New Haven, CT: Relief Book Publishing Company, 1892.

———. *Our Police Protectors: History of the New York Police from the Earliest Period to the Present Time.* Montclair, NJ: Patterson Smith, 1885, 1972.

Crime and Punishment Museum. Washington, D.C., September 16, 2011.

Crisp, Kimberly E. "Water Street Remembered." Honor's thesis, University of New Hampshire–Durham, May 15, 1996.

Cunningham, Mark J. Sammons, and Valerie Cunningham. *Black Portsmouth.* Durham, NH: University Press of New England, 2004.

Cunningham, Valerie. "History of Black Women in Portsmouth, NH." *Portsmouth Discover,* May 4, 2013.

BIBLIOGRAPHY

Dandurant, Karen. "Mayor Badger Runs Prostitutes Out of Town." *Portsmouth Herald*, December 9, 2011.

Dover Gazette. "Letter to the Editor." March 4, 1848.

Duffin, Allan T. *History in Blue*. New York: Kaplan Publishing, 2010.

1890 City of Portsmouth Report. Portsmouth, NH: City of Portsmouth, 1890.

Feals, Jennifer. "City Schools Seek to Restore Painting of Benjamin Franklin." *Portsmouth Herald*, May 23, 2011.

Fielding, John. *An Account of the Origin and Effects of a Police Set on Foot by His Grace the Duke of Newcastle in the Year 1753, upon a Plan Presented to His Grace by the Late Henry Fielding*. London: ECCO Print Editions, 1753.

Goldsmith, Reginald E. *History of the Portsmouth Police Department, 1850–1953*. Portsmouth, NH: self-published, 1953.

Grossman, Nancy W. *The Placenames of Portsmouth*. Portsmouth, NH: Placenames Press, 2005.

Gurney, C.S. *Portsmouth…Historic and Picturesque*. Portland, ME: Lakeside Press, 1902.

Herbert Group Ltd. "Herbert 250 Years." 2010. http://www.herberthistory. co.uk/cgi-bin/sitewise.pl?act=det&p=435 (accessed July 30, 2011).

Hertz, Sue. "Time and Tide in Portsmouth." *Boston Globe Magazine*, April 24, 1983, 12–64.

Inquisition on the Body of a Child Supposed of Ruth Blay. Coroner's report. Concord: New Hampshire Division of Archives and Record Management, June 14, 1768.

International Association of Chiefs of Police. "About the IACP." 2011. http://www.theiacp.org/About/tabid/57/Default.aspx   (accesssed September 5, 20011).

International Publishing Company. *Leading Manufacturers and Merchants of New Hampshire; Historical and Descriptive Review of the Industrial Enterprises of Portsmouth, Great Falls, Concord, Rochester, Nashua, Laconia, Dover, Manchester, Keene and Claremont*. Chicago: International Publishing Company, 1886.

Johnson, David R. *American Law Enforcement: A History*. Wheeling, IL: Forum Press, Inc., 1981.

Knoblock, Glenn A. *Portsmouth Cemeteries*. Portsmouth, NH: Arcadia Publishing, 2005.

Laighton, Albert. "Black Cat Poems: 'The Ballad of Ruth Blay.'" 2007. http://www.blackcatpoems.com/l/the_ballad_of_ruth_blay.html (accessed June 5, 2011).

Lawson, Russell M. *Portsmouth: An Old Town by the Sea*. Charleston, SC: Arcadia Publishing, 2003.

Lockridge, Kenneth A. *A New England Town: The First Hundred Years*. New York: W.W. Norton & Company, 1970.

Lyford, James Otis. *History of the Town of Canterbury, New Hampshire, 1727–1912*. Concord, NH: Rumford Press, 1912.

BIBLIOGRAPHY

MacNamara, Donald E.J. *American Police Administration at Mid-Century.* N.p.: Blackwell Publishing on behalf of the American Society for Public Administration, 1950.

Marvin, Carolyn. *Hanging Ruth Blay: An Eighteenth-Century New Hampshire Tragedy.* Charleston, SC: The History Press, 2010.

Mercer Goodrich, Portsmouth justice of the peace. *Subpoena List for the Coroner's Inquest on the Death of William Canty.* Subpoena. Retrieved from the New Hampshire Division of Archives and Records Management. Portsmouth, NH: Mercer Goodrich, 1876.

Metropolitan Police. "History of the Metropolitan Police." 2011. Metropolitan Police: Working Together for a Safer London. http://www.met.police.uk/history/archives.htm (accessed January 25, 2011).

New Hampshire Gazette and Historical Chronicle, January 27, 1764; September 23, 1768; January 6, 1769.

New Hampshire Public Television. "Our New Hampshire: Portsmouth Summary." September 30, 2005.

New Hampshire secretary of state. "Charter of the Portsmouth Police Commission." April 2, 1895.

New Hampshire Sentinel. "List of Public Executions in New Hampshire." January 21, 1836.

Pearson, Bob. *Murder by Moonlight on the Isle of Shoals.* Concord: Concord, New Hampshire Country Club, May 3, 2013.

Pender, Hon. Thomas Entwistle, and Hon. John Pender. *Career of Two Bobbin Boys.* Portsmouth, NH, 1910.

Penhallow, Samuel, Esq. *The History of the Wars of New England with the Eastern Indians.* Boston: T. Fleet, 1726.

Peterson, Harold Leslie. *Arms and Armor in Colonial America, 1526–1783.* Toronto, ON: General Publishing Company, 2000.

Portsmouth Daily Chronicle. "The Canty Inquest." March 17, 1976.

———. "The Case of Officer Smith." March 18, 1876.

———. "Fatal Affray." March 16, 1876.

———. "Jottings." May 3, 1876.

———. "Officer Smith Case." April 18, 1876.

Portsmouth Daily Evening News. "The Homicide." March 17, 1876.

———. "Jottings." May 3, 1876.

———. "Local Matters." March 21, 1876.

Portsmouth Gazette. "THE DRAFT; A Riot in Portsmouth, N.H. Prompt Dispersion of the Rioters." July 16, 1863.

Portsmouth Herald. "Acting Captain of the Watch Marden Assigned a Beat." January 8, 1898.

———. "Advertisement: Fairbanks Washing Powder." January 3, 1898.

———. August 10, 1895.

———. "Battered Corpse of Marine Found." March 27, 1911.

———. "Ganson Not Guilty." May 13, 1911.

———. "Grand Jury Reported Today." October 19, 1911.

———. "Jack the Hugger." May 5, 1911.

———. March 30, 1895.

———. "Market Street Saloons Hit." April 7, 1911.

———. "Nine Chinamen Captured in Raid." July 17, 1911.

———. "No Bluejackets in Holiday Parade." May 18, 1911.

———. "No Card Playing in Policemen's Recreation Room." July 1, 1911.

———. "Police Have General Shakeup." April 1, 1911.

———. "Police Officer Murphy Stabbed." July 31, 1911.

———. "Police to War on Gambling." July 27, 1911.

Portsmouth Journal. "Cry Baby Tactics." April 6, 1895.

———. February 23, 1895.

———. "A Fresh Start." May 18, 1895.

———. November 30, 1895.

———. October 26, 1895.

Portsmouth Naval Shipyard. *Cradle of American Shipbuilding: History of the Portsmouth Naval Shipyard.* Kittery, ME: Portsmouth Naval Shipyard, 1978.

"Portsmouth Naval Shipyard History." http://www.navsea.navy.mil/shipyards/portsmouth/Pages/History.aspx (accessed September 26, 2010).

Portsmouth Police Commission. Minutes of the Portsmouth Police Commission Meeting, April 1895–June 1905.

Portsmouth Police Court. "Bail Hearing of Andrew J. Smith and Court Order." March 17, 1876

———. *Court Order of Andrew J. Smith.* March 20, 1876.

Portsmouth Police Department Court Log, 1873–1882.

Portsmouth Town Records, 1695–1779. Portsmouth: Sponsored by the City Council of Portsmouth and the University of New Hampshire under the Works Projects Administrator Official Project No. 65-1-13-2098, 1695–1779.

Receipts and Expenditures of the City of Portsmouth for the Year Ending December 31, 1877. Reports of City Officers. Portsmouth, NH: Charles W. Gardner, 1878.

Receipts and Expenditures of the City of Portsmouth for the Year Ending December 31, 1895. Report of City Officers. Portsmouth, NH: Chronicle and Gazette Publishing Company, 1896.

Robinson, J. Dennis. *A Brief History of Portsmouth, New Hampshire.* Portsmouth, NH: Portsmouth Historical Society, 1998.

———. "The Combat Zone, Portsmouth Water Street." SeacoastNH.com. 1998.

———. "The Newspaper Riot of 1865." SeacoastNH.com. 1996.

———. "Seacoast History Blog #52." SeacoastNH.com. 2009.

————. "The Sudden Death of Molly Bridget: Witchery, Spells, Accident, Animals." SeaCoastNH.com. 1999.

————. "Thomsons Were the First NH Settlers in 1623." SeacoastNH. com. 2009.

————. "The Tragic Story of Ruth Blay." SeacoastNH.com. 1999.

Roger Williams University. "Police Chiefs' Forum: Command Institute." Portsmouth, NH, November 18, 2011.

Roth, Mitchel P. *Historical Dictionary of Law Enforcement.* Westport, CT: Greenwood Press, 2001.

Sanborn, Edwin D. *History of New Hampshire from Its First Discovery.* Manchester, NH: John B. Clarke, 1875.

Shi, George Brown Tindall, and David E. Shi. *America: A Narrative History.* 6th edition. New York: W.W. Norton & Company, Inc., 2004.

State of New Hampshire Historical Socity. "Roadside Historical Marker."

Strawbery Banke Museum. "History of Strawbery Banke." September 30, 2005. http://www.strawberybanke.org/museum/history.html.

Toronto Police Service. September 26, 2010. http://www.torontopolice. on.ca/publications/files/misc/history/1t.html.

Towne of Portsmouth Records, 1645–1713. Official Town Records, Typescript copy. Portsmouth, NH: Works Projects Administrator Official Project No. 65-1-13-2098, 1645-1713.

United States Geological Service. "USGS Earthquake History." October 21, 2009. http://earthquake.usgs.gov/earthquakes/states/vermont/ history.php (accessed May 27, 2011).

United States Navy. "History of the Portsmouth Naval Shipyard." 2011. http://www.navsea.navy.mil/shipyards/portsmouth/Pages/History.aspx (accessed July 30, 2011).

Unknown. "The Early Police Force of Portsmouth: The Volunteer Men of 1811." N.d.

Vila, Bryan, and Cynthia Morris. *The Role of Police in American Society.* Westport, CT: Greenwood Press, 1999.

The Warner House Association. "The Warner House: A Rich and Colorful History." Portsmouth, NH: Warner House Association, 2006.

Winslow, Ola Elizabeth. *Portsmouth: The Life of a Town.* New York: Macmillan Company, 1966.

Winthrop, John. *The History of New England from 1630 to 1649.* Boston: James Savage edition, 1853.

The Winthrop Society. "The Memoir of Capt. Roger Clapp of Dorchester ca. 1640." 1996–2003. http://www.winthropsociety.com/doc_clapp.php (accessed March 29, 2011).

ABOUT THE AUTHOR

Dr. David "Lou" Ferland
Portsmouth, New Hampshire Chief of Police (Ret.)
Mount Washington College

D r. David J. Ferland, or "Lou" to most, was a police officer with the 110-person Portsmouth Police Department for thirty years. He acquired his doctoral degree from Franklin Pierce University, writing his dissertation on "Crime, Punishment and the History of the Portsmouth, N.H. Police Department."

Dr. Ferland is a nationally certified police K-9 trainer/judge and was head trainer of the New Hampshire Police K-9 Academy for ten years.

He has received many awards, both locally and nationally, and is a highly rated public speaker and teacher on leadership issues,

The author in a reproduction 1880 Portsmouth Police uniform depicted in a daguerreotype photo. *Author's collection.*

criminal justice, public policy, police K-9 and police history. He lives in Portsmouth with Lynda and their daughter, Justine. He can be reached by e-mail at DavidFerlandK9@gmail.com.